Hovering Over Baja

Hovering Over Baja

by

Erle Stanley Gardner

William Morrow and Company
New York 1961

Contents

Illustrations

Hovering Over Baja

#1

Introducing the Pak-Jak

I have been exploring Baja California for many years. I thought I knew something about it. I have a whole fleet of four-wheel drive automobiles and from time to time we had made excursions down the rough, narrow roads of the peninsula to the various points of interest: to Bahia de Los Angeles, the fishing paradise; to Scammon's Lagoon, the breeding place of the whales; to the fabulous Hattie Hamilton Ranch a hundred odd miles below Ensenada; to the Sky Ranch at San Quintin, the home of the most wonderful clams and then on beyond to Santa Rosalia, Mulegé and El Coyote; to San José del Cabo, La Paz and to the Cape. In short, I had pretty much worn a series of ruts in the road and thought I knew the country pretty well.

Then at a time when I was looking for new adventures, my friend J. W. Black of Paradise designed the Pak-Jak.

The Pak-Jak is something of a cross between a motor-cycle, a scooter and an army tank.

At the time Black designed his machine there were other devices on the market, but they didn't appeal to Black as being just what he wanted.

Black wanted something that was so rugged in construction that it would be almost indestructible. He wanted something so thoroughly dependable that a man could rely on it in places where his very life would be forfeit if there should be a mechanical failure. He also wanted something that had enough power to go just as straight up as a rider could sit in the saddle without having the whole contraption fall over backwards. And he wanted something that weighed under a hundred and seventy-five pounds gross.

It took quite a bit of inventing to come up with a machine that satisfied Black, but eventually he did so and called it the Pak-Jak.

Because Black was a friend of mine, I was in on the ground floor, so to speak, of all the experimentation and designing and almost immediately I dreamed up an idea for an adventure de luxe.

We would take half a dozen of these machines. Black would design a two-wheeled trailer which could be pulled by the machine and which would carry five or six hundred pounds of camping equipment on reasonably level ground.

We would go by boat down the coast of Baja California taking these Pak-Jaks with us, would unload the outfit at Guerrero Negro and would then start moving up the beaches. We would travel with the trailers at low tide, keeping to the hard-packed sand. Then as the tide came in and we had to move up the beach to where the sand became softer, we would disconnect the trailers and use the Pak-Jaks to explore the back country until once more the tide went down and we could find a sandy strip of hard beach sufficiently wide and

The author on his Pak-Jak.

J. W. Black.

firm to enable the trailers and camp outfit to be transported.

The idea was simple enough and sound enough, provided the beaches would adapt themselves to this type of exploration.

We knew, of course, that the extent of sandy beaches was the vital factor in our plan. We realized that from time to time there were jagged promontories cropping out into the ocean which would present effective barriers to further progress even at low tide.

However, after seeing the versatility of Black's contraption and the terrain over which he was able to navigate successfully, I had high hopes that by picking the right stretch of beach we could perhaps have as much as fifty miles of exploration, and that our excursions into the back country would unearth material which would be of great interest: evidence of prehistoric Indian villages, perhaps even an unexpected water hole. At that time, I was under the impression that Baja California was pretty much of a desert. Certainly anyone who traverses the road is entitled to reach that assumption.

While there are a few well-watered oases such as the beautiful palm-covered country of San Ignacio, the road for the most part goes through a dry, arid country where anyone on foot would almost inevitably perish of thirst before he could reach any human habitation or any source of drinking water.

We also wanted to make a survey of the country to see to what extent it was populated by game.

I had seen enough of the beaches near Guerrero Negro to know that it would be possible to go some distance with our Pak-Jaks and trailers and I felt certain we could have adventure and probably explore country where no tourist had ever set foot.

However, we wanted to make certain.

J. W. Black constructed his trailers and tested them out so that he was satisfied we could carry quite a supply of camp goods, drinking water, gasoline, sleeping bags and provisions along reasonably level country. All that was needed now was to pick out the particular beach that we wanted to explore.

Quite obviously the best way to do that was by air.

Baja California has generated a breed of pilots which is comparable to the bush pilots of Canada and Alaska.

These men bring lobsters from the lobster camps into the market. Quite obviously lobsters have to be transported when they are ready to go and the market is ready to receive them. Adverse weather conditions, including wind, must not be a deterrent, yet Baja California is often the scene of great turbulence in the mountains and fog on the beaches.

So these Baja California pilots learn to fly by instinct, the seat of their pants, an inherent skill and a daring resourcefulness which puts them out in front as the world's best and most daring fliers.

My friend Francisco Munoz is one of these pilots. He has now graduated from flying lobsters and has a regular passenger service from Tijuana to the Bahia de Los Angeles, but he also has time to do some charter flying. So I contacted Francisco Munoz and made arrangements for an exploratory trip at a time when he would have two full days at his disposal.

Sam Hicks, my assistant and ranch manager, J. W. Black, inventor of the Pak-Jak, Murl Emery, a rugged desert prospector who is one of the greatest living authorities on Baja California, and I crowded into the plane with Munoz and we took off from Tijuana.

There are two sections of Baja California: the north and the south. And the northern state is, in turn, divided into two very definite sections, although there is no actual demarcation other than the one political boundary which is merely a surveyed line.

Mexicali, the capital of the state, is a thriving, prosperous city that is growing so fast it is bursting out at the seams.

Over to the west, Tijuana, which was once considered to be purely a city of vice, is becoming a center of legitimate entertainment, with its race track, bull ring, jai alai, and it, too, is growing like a mushroom.

When I first knew the city, it consisted of only a few adobe buildings and one unpaved street. Today it is a prosperous city of a hundred and sixty-five thousand people with scores of legitimate tourist attractions. There is a constant flow of commerce back and forth across the border and it plays an important part in the economy both of California to the north and of Baja California to the south.

Heaven knows how many tourists go to San Diego simply to make the trip across to Tijuana in Mexico—tourists who would never have gone farther south than Los Angeles if it hadn't been for colorful Tijuana.

Munoz has a single-motored airplane which he keeps in the pink of condition, since he spends much of his life flying over mountains so rough that an engine failure would mean almost inevitable disaster.

There are two schools of thought about this flying over rough terrain: one is that two motors are better than one, and that is undoubtedly sound reasoning.

The other school of thought, however, is that with a single-motored plane and its slower landing speed, one stands a much better chance, in case one does have to make a forced landing, of walking away from the plane. And, of course, there are other factors involved, such as operational economies, etc.

In any event, Munoz has a single-motored plane and since he realizes the importance of keeping that plane in good condition, I always feel pretty much at ease when I am flying with him.*

On this trip, Munoz was going to take us exploring. We weren't going to follow any established routes, nor were we going to play it safe. We were going up into the mountains to the south of Tijuana and to the east of Ensenada in order to see some country that Munoz thought we might be interested in, although I felt at the time that it had to be the beaches or nothing. We weren't interested in mountain canyons. However, since the country between Tijuana and Ensenada is traversed by a paved road, we didn't care about the beaches until after we had passed the Hattie Hamilton Ranch some hundred and twenty miles to the south of Ensenada.

Ensenada, by the way, has emerged from a sleepy little Mexican village and is now a thriving port with facilities for both large and small craft, excellent accommodations for the tourist, and is populated by some of the most forward-looking, alert businessmen one could hope to meet anywhere.

This is a good thing for the economy of Baja California and a good thing for the United States. Yet I look back with nostalgic memories on the time when Ensenada was merely a very, very colorful Mexican town, with its fuel delivered daily by burros who were driven in from the hinterland where wood choppers loaded them with firewood, made the long trip to Ensenada and then turned the burros loose at night to clatter along the sidewalks looking for shrubs on which they could browse.

However, as has been so aptly remarked, one can't eat his cake and have it too.

As the Mexicans say, "One door never closes but another opens," and over on the gulf side of the peninsula a hundred and twenty miles below Mexicali, the fishing village of San

*Since this was written, Munoz has added a twin-motor plane to his equipment.

Francisco Munoz, who uses "Body English" with his face when putting an idea across.

Felipe will give the tourist all that he wants in the way of local color with quite good motel and restaurant facilities thrown in. There are also fishing boats that can take the tourist out into semitropical waters where there is first-class fishing.

One of the outstanding citizens of Ensenada is David Zarate Zazueta. (Usually when a Mexican gentleman has three names, he is called by the middle name. The last name is the name of his mother.) "Dave" Zarate has for many years been a colorful and influential figure in Baja California.

There is a custom that the mayor is not to be re-elected for a second consecutive term. The next most influential position in the city is that of president of the chamber of commerce.

So for many years Zarate was alternately mayor of the city, then president of the chamber of commerce, then would again be elected as mayor of the city.

Dave is virtually bilingual and has a polished charm which is distinctive, yet difficult to describe.

While there is a certain formal undertone, yet it is so utterly sincere and natural that it lacks any touch of affectation, and fits the man's personality as easily as a well-worn shoe or perhaps it would be better to say a well-worn glove. It is to some extent quite typical of the Mexican gentleman.

Dave is one of those individuals who has what can only be described for want of a better name as intellectual perspective. He meets everyone on the common ground of mutual understanding. I have known him for some thirty-five years and find that his name inspires tremendous respect both in Baja California and among the people who know him north of the border.

Above all Dave Zarate is a great friend, warm, loyal and interesting. It is always a pleasure to visit with him.

Yet Señor Zarate is only one of the outstanding citizens

of Ensenada. I mention him particularly because of my long years of friendship.

This little city of Ensenada has some of the most progressive citizens of any of the Baja California cities. As one of my friends recently expressed it, "If you want to get something done in Baja California, go to Ensenada. If it's anything worth while they'll get back of it, and if they get back of it they'll get results."

Looking back on it, I think Munoz realized that our dream of exploring the beaches of Baja California was impractical, and wanted to direct our attention to some of the other country which was completely unknown as far as the tourist was concerned. In fact, this country is completely unknown to everyone except a small handful of people: aviators who have flown over it, mostly at great height because of the rugged nature of the country beneath; a few prospectors who have apparently been in some of the country at one time or another; and one or two ranchers whose cattle have strayed into some of these canyons and who have followed them at least for a short distance before giving up the chase.

So after leaving Tijuana, Munoz set a course which would bring us into country which I never knew existed.

Years ago, my friend Goldbaum of Ensenada, who was a great Mexican patriot and an enthusiastic booster for the peninsula, had assured me that Baja California had a lot more water than people realized, that back in unexplored sections of the peninsula were palm-lined canyons where there was running water, deep crystal-clear pools carved out of the solid granite, and a land of virgin fertility.

Goldbaum had made several mule-back trips into the "back country" trying to find out more about it. He carried a sextant with him and would shoot the sun at noon, pricking his position on a chart and then taking photographs which were identified by longitude and latitude.

HOVERING OVER BAJA

He had a museum at Ensenada in which he had many curios, many Indian artifacts and books filled with photographs.

Much of what he had told me was more or less hazy in my mind because at the time I was more interested in the very remarkable man than in the things he had found; but some of the things he had said had stuck in my mind and now began to come back as Munoz, flying over country where no single-motored airplane had any business, began to show us far, far below, canyons that undoubtedly were studded with palm trees and in which there was a plentiful supply of water.

These things simply weren't supposed to exist in Baja California. It was supposed to be an arid desert region with an incomparable climate; warm, dry air; plenty of sunshine; and more days of sunlight than any place in the Southwest other than the arid desert regions.

Munoz knew we wanted to fly low enough to see the canyons, but he also is a prudent flier and he knew that he

From this high altitude there appeared to be palm trees in this valley, and the strong probability of water.

couldn't afford to take any unnecessary chances. Flying over that country in the first place was taking plenty of chances.

So we broke out our cameras and started taking photographs, incredulously studying the terrain below and wondering how we could possibly get into it.

Munoz circled and flew us to a point where we could see the nearest road. Then we took photographs of landmarks fixing the locations in our minds and on photographic film so that we could find our way back by four-wheel drive automobile to the end of the road, and then by using Pak-Jaks could head in over the game trails which led from the dry mesa country down to the watered canyons.

By the time we had finished exploring the country back in those mountains and had headed for the ocean below San Quintin, we were so tremendously excited that when it began to be apparent our dream of exploring the beaches with Pak-Jaks was impractical, we weren't too badly disappointed.

So we asked Munoz if there were any more canyons that he knew about and he told us there were vast sections of the mountain country which were virtually unexplored. He had, he said, flown high over other canyons where he felt certain there was water and in one place had seen what looked like ruins of a huge building.

Then he told us about the canyons of La Asamblea and Sal Si Puede.

I don't know what is the significance of the name La Asamblea, but Sal Si Puede being literally translated means "get out if you can."

These are two main canyons in a series of canyons to the north of Bahia de Los Angeles and there are some interesting stories connected with them.

From the air, the canyons look like the branches of coral, winding perhaps twenty-five miles up from the gulf into the granite mountains.

No tourist has ever explored these canyons. A few hard-bitten Mexican prospectors have from time to time landed at the beach on the gulf side during periods of calm weather and by walking up the sandy wash have covered the four or five miles of terrain to the place where the canyons begin. Then they have gone an undetermined distance up the canyons, but no one has ever gone very far, at least up Sal Si Puede.

There is supposed to be a spring of good water in La Asamblea about twelve miles from the ocean, and there are stories of people who have reached that spring of water and managed to return. There are also stories of people who lost their lives in the attempt.

So having flown down to the south along the coastline until we became convinced that there were no beaches to the north of Guerrero Negro of sufficient extent to satisfy our purpose, we asked Munoz to fly us over the gulf side of the peninsula so we could take a look at the palm-lined canyons to the north of Bahia de Los Angeles.

We spent that night at Bahia de Los Angeles, a resort operated by my friend Antero Diaz and his wife; a place which is utterly unique.

This place is only some three hours flight from the congested district of Los Angeles and San Diego. It is known to scores of sportsmen having private planes, and on weekends plane after plane will come in bringing adventurous fishermen or people who simply want to make the trip and relax in the warm sunshine off the gulf, or perhaps get in a little fishing; but above all, to sample the fabulous cooking prepared under the direction of Señora Diaz.

The table has delicacies which would satisfy a gourmet and are so tastefully prepared and in such quantities that it is difficult for appetites sharpened by the tang of salt air and the balmy breezes to realize that there is any stopping point.

Meals consist of steaks from the big gulf turtles, abalone, fillets of freshly caught sea bass, shrimp fresh from the water, lobsters, tortillas, frijoles and perhaps most surprising of all, fresh, crisp salads.

There are large cabins with wide, spacious porches on which one can sit and look out over the gulf. There is indoor plumbing. The beds are good, the people friendly and the service excellent, but there is warm water only when the sun shines during the middle of the day or the first part of the afternoon.

Water from a huge spring above the resort is piped into fifty gallon drums on the roofs of the cabins. The sun warms this water during the middle of the day and the first part of the afternoon so that it comes out of the shower perhaps a little better than lukewarm. But the person who hopes to take a shower early in the morning or late at night, had better prepare himself for a shock as he steps into the little cemented alcove off his bathroom and turns on the single faucet.

There is, however, such a charm about the place that people who have been there keep coming back. Antero is never at a loss for customers. Sometimes there may be only five or six; sometimes there may be fifty, but the facilities are equal to the occasion. Everybody will be fed and bedded, and for those who want to fish, there will be plenty of boats and plenty of fish, together with all the guides that are necessary.

Of late Diaz has added an eighty foot twin-screwed Diesel boat to his fleet. This boat is a converted sub chaser and there are reasonably comfortable quarters for sportsmen who wish to go far out into the gulf, over to the east side of the island of Angel de La Guarda where there are some of the most flavorful oysters in the world to be had for the taking, where there are big clams and where the fishing is out of this world.

Antero Diaz, an intelligent organizer and executive.

We had an enjoyable night with our friends there at the Bahia de Los Angeles and then the next morning Munoz started us on a flight which was to have a far-reaching effect on my future.

We flew up to the palm-lined canyons and explored them as well as we could from the height which we had to maintain in order to have any reasonable standard of safety.

Looking down on those canyons, it was easy to see why they were unexplored.

On the gulf side was a rather rugged beach where breakers stretched far out whenever there was any wind. Only during periods of dead calm would it be practical to land a boat laden with supplies on this beach.

Back from the beach was a stretch of some five miles of deep sand running up a barren wash where some of the most colorful mountains I had ever seen were spread haphazardly on each side of the wash.

These mountains had various strata of all different colors: red, pink, green, and various pastel shades. They were for the most part completely devoid of vegetation and down in the wash below where one must walk through ankle-deep sand, the sun beat down with pitiless intensity and the sand threw back the rays and the heat so that even in mid-winter a person who would walk up that wash must wear heavy dark glasses, carry plenty of water in his canteen and move slowly.

About five miles up from the ocean, the canyons began, starting out as two main canyons and then branching out into dozens of canyons which ran back into the granite mountains.

Those mountains were great piles of granite boulders varying in size from small rocks to those the size of a skyscraper, tumbled in confusion with precipices to trap the unwary traveler.

It would be impossible for any man to walk over these

mountains. If he carried plenty of ropes, he could, of course, make a mountain climbing project of it and eventually and gradually get down or up these slopes.

However, there was not just one single range of these mountains but wave on wave of mountain ranges, consisting of granite, and in places mile after mile of tumbled malpais boulders, a particularly hard iron-colored, exceedingly heavy volcanic formation.

The mere sight of those mountains even from high up in the air, gave one the shivers. Apparently the only practical way into the canyons was up from the wash on the gulf side.

However, Munoz wanted to show us a route he had worked out which he thought might be practical for Pak-Jaks.

Some fifteen miles back from the gulf, there was a series of dry lakes, and Munoz felt that four-wheel drive automobiles with skillful drivers could manage to get into these dry lakes. He also felt that he could arrange to land on one of these lakes, particularly if an automobile on the ground marked out a smooth strip which would be free of "pot holes."

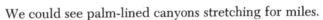

We could see palm-lined canyons stretching for miles.

From that point, it was only some six miles over to a section of the Sal Si Puede Canyon and the mountains were rather low and not quite so precipitous.

Munoz thought we might be able to establish a base camp on this dry lake and get our Pak-Jaks over the mountains and down into the canyon.

Munoz was about the only one who thought so.

Yet the canyons represented a continuing challenge. I couldn't get them out of my mind.

Persons who lived in Bahia de Los Angeles and were familiar with the country assured me that no one had been up in them for at least eighteen years to their positive knowledge.

From time to time, people landed from fishing boats during periods of calm and explored the wash and an occasional hardy soul had even got up to the canyons themselves. One man was reputed to have gone up La Asamblea Canyon to the spring of good water and had managed to return the following day.

There was one most interesting story about La Asamblea Canyon.

Twenty-eight years ago two prospectors landed on the beach and trudged up the sandy wash until they came to the mouth of the canyons. Then they started prospecting up the canyon.

It was agreed that one man would take all of the food and water and try to prospect while his companion went back to the boat to replenish supplies and return to join forces with the prospector.

On returning to the place selected as a rendezvous, the man who was laden with provisions and all the water he could carry, found no trace of his companion. He waited impatiently with time rapidly running out, then started exploring trying to find the tracks of his companion.

Eventually he found his partner. He had been bitten by a rattlesnake and had died a horrible death. The story was pathetically told in the man's rolled-up trouser leg, the tourniquet he had placed around his leg above the bite, and the knife slashes he had made in his leg.

It should be mentioned parenthetically that this section of the country is the home of a very rare, very vicious and very deadly rattlesnake: a red diamondback, which attains lengths up to six feet and the poison is so deadly that there is no known instance of a person who has been bitten surviving to report the symptoms.

There is one exception: some time ago a herpetologist handling one of these rattlesnakes in a museum, received a glancing blow on the leg. Nearly all of the venom ran down his pants' leg to the floor, but a small amount got into the blood stream.

This man was in a hospital within seventeen minutes after having been bitten; he was given all of the treatment that modern science knew about. He had anti-venom serum; he had antibiotics; medicine for the heart; morphine for the nerves. He had everything.

Yet this man nearly died. He had taken with him a pad and pencil intending to write down his symptoms, because he recognized the scientific value of doing so, but he was too ill to make even a single note.

And it is to be remembered that this snake struck only a glancing blow. He struck blind through the folds of a sack, all but missed the man's leg, and spilled nearly all the venom on the floor.

Any man who is bitten by one of these red diamondback rattlesnakes where the fangs penetrate deeply and the full dose of venom goes into the blood stream, might just as well give up.

To get back to our prospector, however, when his body

was discovered, it was found that he was without his prospector's pick.

Since a prospector's pick to a prospector in that canyon would have been at least as important as his canteen of water, it was assumed that when the snake had buried his fangs in the man's leg, the man had lashed down with the prospector's pick, breaking loose the snake's hold. And as he had done so, the pick had slipped out of his hands. The snake presumably was killed, or at least his fangs had been removed from the man's leg and the man had no time to pick up the prospector's pick, but was busily engaged in trying to save his life.

The interesting thing, however, was that around the man's shoulder was a sack containing ore.

Stories vary as to the richness of this ore. Some people say simply that it was very rich; others say that it was almost pure gold.

The surviving partner had hurried back down the wash, had got in his boat and gone to Bahia de Los Angeles for help. Then because the weather was calm they were able to return to the canyon and bury his partner. And, of course, there was a great deal of excitement over the sack of rich ore which had been on the man's shoulder. He had discovered a mineral deposit of fabulous richness.

Thereafter, four people lost their lives trying to get into this canyon to search for gold.

Would the Pak-Jak enable us to get up these canyons and explore them? Could we use this interesting device to get into places where no tourist had ever been, or could ever hope to go by using ordinary means of transportation?

We made several surveys from the air and became convinced that if we could land on the beach, the Pak-Jaks would pull our trailers loaded with provisions up to the canyons themselves. We could establish a base camp here and

Munoz, who has spent most of his life flying over rough terrain.

have at least one or two days of exploration ahead of us before having to get back down to the beach.

And, of course, we realized that we couldn't land at all during periods of high wind and that when we got ready to come home, we might find ourselves marooned down on the beach.

There was also the realization that if anything went wrong, we were going to add our names to the list of those who had given up their lives trying to explore the deadly canyons.

So after Munoz had circled the canyons several times and we had taken pictures, we headed on north, where Munoz showed us other parts of the peninsula which he felt certain had never known the foot of a tourist and many places where, aside from prehistoric Indians, it was quite probable no human foot had ever trod.

All in all, when we returned to Tijuana with a map showing dozens of places that we wanted to explore, we were filled with excitement.

We all agreed that the first objective we should have was that of the twin canyons of La Asamblea and Sal Si Puede and the numerous branches that fanned out into the granite country.

So we arranged with Antero Diaz to charter his eighty foot boat on which we could load our Pak-Jaks, trailers and provisions, and we wanted some smaller boats equipped with powerful outboard motors to keep with us, so that in the event of any emergency we could launch a speedboat and get back down to the Bahia de Los Angeles.

Antero had a healthy respect for those canyons. In addition to our other precautions, he insisted that we carry with us a compact battery-powered, but very powerful, radio so that he could keep in touch with us at the Bahia de Los Angeles.

Every day at noon we were to try and call him and report whether we were okay and whether we needed anything. If, because of static or other trouble, we couldn't get him at noon, we were to try again at five o'clock in the evening and if that failed, we were to try at six o'clock the next morning.

In addition to all of these other precautions, Munoz was to fly over us if we ever actually got into the wash, keeping an eye on us and in case we got into any real trouble and needed anything, we worked out an elaborate system of signals by which we could make our wants known.

So we hurriedly assembled a caravan to go down the road from Mexicali to Bahia de Los Angeles; a caravan that would carry Pak-Jaks, trailers, sleeping bags, food, gasoline, water cans, some tents for our base camp, and, of course, plenty of cameras and film.

Then we started out, filled with determination to get into those canyons, or else.

#2

The Road to Bahia

Baja California is the scene of an ancient civilization. It is a fabulous country, rich in history, rich in mystery. It is a land of almost perpetual sunshine; the ocean is warm and blue, while the air, despite its proximity to the ocean, is dry and clear.

Murl Emery tells me that scientific research shows that up until about three hundred years ago the peninsula was well watered; and history shows that it supported a large number of Indians. Then came the period of drouth. The ground slowly turned to desert. The Indians died off.

No one knows why these things happen, why these basic changes take place in climate, but the evidence shows that they do.

While cars with two-wheel drive *have* been taken over the road from Mexicali to Bahia de Los Angeles, it is not advisable for anyone to start out on the trip unless he is an experienced desert driver, has a car equipped with four-wheel drive, *or* a pickup with four-speed transmission, a properly balanced load, and is accompanied by a car which has four-wheel drive and a tow chain for short sandy stretches or emergencies.

Nor is it really advisable for one person to make the trip alone, nor for any number to make a trip in one car. It is better to have two cars and one should carry plenty of drinking water and gasoline.

We paused in Mexicali long enough to say hello to Joe and Emily Gutierrez.

Colonel José Gutierrez is typical of the best of Mexico, a man with driving energy, a keen sense of humor, shrewd business acumen and great loyalty to his friends. He lives a very rich life and for many years he has been my friend.

He and Emily (born in the United States) have an international marriage that has really worked out. Whenever I go to Mexico via Calexico and Mexicali, I look forward to a visit with these friends.

Gutierrez is always building up a business of some sort. The man is a dynamo of creative and executive energy, and I sometimes think he likes to engage in new enterprises just for the sheer pleasure of overcoming seemingly insurmountable obstacles.

His hobby is training jumping horses.

He loves horses and has great skill in training them. Recently a friend of his had an "outlaw" horse which he was threatening to kill. Colonel Gutierrez told the friend this would be a mistake so the friend said, "All right, I'll give *you* the horse. Let's see what *you* can do with him."

So Joe took the horse and a few weeks later the animal would let Joe climb all over him, crawl under him, ride him anywhere.

Recently Joe has gone into the bottling business—having the franchise for Orange Crush. This is something of a sideline with him, but his plant is a huge modern bottling works sparklingly clean. The drink is distributed by a fleet of trucks and the plant is a credit to Mexicali.

It was therefore only natural that when we left Mexicali our cars would be loaded with case after case of Orange Crush—a "going away" present from Joe Gutierrez who had taken a half day out of his busy schedule to see that we got across the border without undue delay and got started on our trip under favorable auspices.

From Mexicali the road is surfaced to San Felipe, which is one hundred twenty miles south of the Border.

San Felipe is a fishing camp-tourist resort, which is becoming better known and more popular day by day. There are boats to be rented here, there are good stores, there is a very fine motel, a superb restaurant and a most interesting curio store specializing in leather goods.

There is also a bakery which makes some of the best rolls I have ever tasted. I don't know what there is about the Mexican flour and the Mexican way of cooking which imparts such flavor to the products of the Mexican bakeries, but the fact remains that there is all the difference in the world between a roll cooked in the bake shop at San Felipe and one served in the most high-priced restaurants in the United States. Whenever we pass through San Felipe we get a big pasteboard carton filled with these rolls.

Most writers of Baja California put in a lot of time describing the road. This is only natural because one who has driven that road has been a very busy individual and he knows he has been places. The road becomes of supreme importance to the average driver and so he becomes completely preoccupied with it. It is like the man who has gone through surgery and wants to tell everybody about his operation.

But, after all, a road is only the means of getting to some place and from time to time the road will vary as work is done on it.

I know that in my first book on Baja California (*The Land of Shorter Shadows*) I described the section of the road on which was a painted skull and crossbones as a warning to everyone using the road. It was known as "The Point of the Picture of Death" and it was exceedingly dangerous.

One of my companions was injured here—as it later turned out, quite seriously.

Shortly after that accident the Mexican Government hired people to improve that section of the road. The rocky, overhanging wall was blasted away. The road was widened and somewhat straightened. The picture of the skull and crossbones remained.

Because I was so impressed by The Point of the Picture of Death, I described it in detail. Yet within three or four months of the time my book appeared in print the road had been changed. Since that time every writer, journeying down Baja California, refers somewhat patronizingly to my concern

A forest of cardones.

at negotiating The Point of the Picture of Death, and comments on how he went around the place without the slightest trouble.

Now the road from San Felipe to Puertecitos, a distance of around fifty-two miles, is subject to more change than any other road in Baja California that I know of.

There are places where the road runs over a hard, rocky alluvial plain and where the surface can be washboarded so it will jar your eyeteeth out. Then it crosses long stretches of sandy wash and I have seen this road so churned up that if you are forced to get over to the side in order to let some other vehicle pass, the chances of getting stuck are very good indeed.

Moreover, American tourists insist upon towing trailers with boats down this stretch of road, and when the road is bad there are tourists stretched all along it in various kinds of trouble—broken trailer hitches, blown-out tires, overheated motors, vapor locks; and, in fact, almost every kind of mechanical ill to which the average motorist is prone, including being just plain stuck in the sand.

However, the Mexicans work this road regularly, and if you come along after it has been repaired it is a breeze. You drift along, averaging almost thirty miles an hour, wondering what would cause anyone the slightest concern in negotiating *this* road.

Two months later you jolt your way over the harder places, churn your way through the sand and think this must be a terrible way to travel.

Puertecitos is an interesting little fishing camp resort. There is a restaurant and a bar built from native rocks which were harvested from the adjoining mountains. On the outside these rocks have been left rugged and jagged, but on the inside they have been cut, smoothed and varnished.

There are boats here and a limited number of persons

can get accommodations. There is good gasoline and a gas pump, and this is the last place one can get gasoline until one comes to the Bahia de Los Angeles, around a hundred and fifty road miles farther south.

Below Puertecitos one suddenly realizes he is in a country where road conditions are somewhat unpredictable. However, here again, I have seen all sorts of changes in the road from time to time. There are times when one can very readily make it in a two-wheel drive pickup with a four-speed transmission. There are times when I wouldn't want to tackle it with anything except a four-wheel drive.

For some thirty miles south of Puertecitos there is a succession of short, steep pitches and a few rather long, narrow grades which are very steep indeed.

The really expert dirt-road driver on coming to one of these grades shifts into low gear and moves slowly and steadily up the road, and if the road is smooth he can get over the summit. The average driver, however, charges at the road with all the speed he can muster, drops into second gear as soon as the pulling gets tough, and then, just before

South of Puertecitos the road winds over a rough, mountainous terrain. It is almost essential to have four-wheel drive automobiles.

How we carried our Pak-Jaks.

he gets to the top, when he encounters the real test of his motor, throws the gearshift lever into his lowest gear and steps on the throttle. The result is that the wheels start to spin, making a little depression in the road for the next car; and, since the second car will find the going getting tough at approximately the same place, its driver will shift his gears and the spinning wheels will make just that much more of a hole. By the time enough cars have been over the road it is all but impassable for two-wheel drive vehicles.

After a while one encounters a whole succession of these holes, the cars will stall, and the unhappy motorists have no alternative but to back slowly, painfully, laboriously and dangerously down the narrow hairpin turns of the grade to a place where there is good footing in order to try it again.

Recently a couple of volunteer road workers have taken over on this stretch and have done marvels with it.

These volunteer road workers are most interesting people. They find there is not enough work to go around. They are hungry, they want to work, and so they have started making their own jobs.

42

They will take a piece of canvas, an old tent, or perhaps just pieces of wrecked automobiles, and go out on the road and establish a base camp, with a few cans to hold drinking water.

These camps are unbelievably primitive, yet always immaculate. The men who refuse to be licked by adverse conditions and go out to carve their own careers are the men who are the true adventurers in this world, the ones who will always manage to get by some way.

These volunteer road workers live under conditions of austerity, in constant hunger. But they put in their time out on the road with pick, shovel and rake, pecking away at filling in loose holes, painfully hauling gravel—sometimes a shovelful at a time—and in general manicuring the road by hand so that it is greatly improved.

The truck drivers who use this stretch of road do so in fear and trembling. One needs only to look at the piles of wreckage down in the canyons alongside these grades to realize the danger.

Almost every time one comes along this road there are evidences of a new wreck, another truck which has gone off the road.

If a truck stalls on one of these grades, trying to back it down the grade for a fresh start is one of the most dangerous feats of driving one could well ask for, and before one gets to the bottom the chances are he will have lost control and started on a wild, careening ride down the grade which will terminate with the car rolling over and over and coming to rest with a crash at the bottom.

So the truck drivers are grateful to these volunteer road workers. Despite the fact the truck driver is apt to be quite poor himself, he can nearly always find some gift for the road worker; a little food, a cigarette and he can fill up the man's water cans.

On this trip I had anticipated some difficulty with the two-wheel drive pickup I took along as we reached the country south of Puertecitos, but the road had been smoothed so that we didn't need to surge on the power. We could keep an even, steady pace and we went up over the steep grades without the slightest difficulty; although on our way back we did encounter a party that was having lots of trouble.

Their plight represented one of the tragedies of Mexico; the lack of capital which besets willing, energetic men who would like to better themselves.

The people in this party were very enterprising, willing workers. They had pooled their resources so they could buy a secondhand truck. Then they had mortgaged the truck to get a stock of staple provisions and with these provisions they had left Mexicali to drive down Baja California, hoping to sell the load at a sufficient profit to enable them to pay out and make a good return on their investment.

Unfortunately, these men were unfamiliar with the roads and when they hit the first of these long grades they realized that the truck probably would not be able to pull the load up the grade, a distance of perhaps a mile of winding, narrow, very steep road. They also saw the wreckage of other trucks down in the canyon at the bottom—a grim reminder that the road could take its toll.

So they played it safe. They unloaded the truck at the bottom of the grade and took it empty to the top. Then by sheer manpower they started carrying the load up the grade.

That would have been an almost endless task, and probably would have been more than the men could have hoped to accomplish.

Yet when we came on them they had carried the first part of the load about two-thirds of the way up the grade,

Puertecitos.

San Felipe.

Typical Baja California scenery.

Cirio trees and cardones.

and it was a terrific job. There were sacks of potatoes that weighed over two hundred pounds. These men had lifted them to their shoulders and were staggering up the grade. There were hundred-pound sacks of flour and tin tubs of lard; things which couldn't be divided and which were exceedingly heavy.

There is one thing about the Mexican driver, when he gets into trouble he has no regard for passing traffic. If he can't go, there is no reason why anyone else should.

So we found the road blocked at the top of the grade by the empty truck, and at the bottom of the grade, by the pile of foodstuffs which had been taken from the truck and left there to be carried up by manpower. We also found the first-backaching consignment of goods about two-thirds of the way up the grade.

Sam Hicks and J. W. Black are rough, rugged individuals. They wanted to show these Mexicans that they could do a job when a job needed to be done, so they walked down and each picked up one of these two-hundred-odd-pound sacks of potatoes, hoisted it to his shoulder and started walking up the grade; a grade so steep that cars with two-wheel drive sometimes stall on it.

It was soon apparent, however, that this method of transporting the load of the truck was going to be simply out of the question. So Sam got the men to move the empty truck at the top, then he turned one of the four-wheel drive pickups around and backed down the grade.

The Mexicans watched this operation with awe.

Backing a truck is an operation which Mexicans are not anxious to undertake, nor do I think they are very good at it. Backing a truck down this steep grade made them apprehensive and they wouldn't even consider riding down the grade but ran all the way down so that they could help load the truck at the bottom.

Sam Hicks.

Sam, who is an expert driver, backed the car around all of the sharp turns, down to the bottom of the grade. Then they loaded about a third of the stuff on the pickup and Sam ran it back up with the aid of four-wheel drive, transferred the load to the Mexicans' truck and then repeated the process on two additional trips so as to finish up all of the load that was at the bottom, leaving the Mexicans jubilant and the road clear.

However, we had to point out that there were grades ahead equally formidable.

I am wondering how those Mexicans got over the rest

of that road, where they are now, and what happened to their load. Even when we found them, two of the sacks had become punctured and flour was leaking out.

When one considers the days of heartbreaking labor which went into amassing the capital necessary for this venture, it is easy to see the inherent tragedy, the almost inevitable financial disaster, which lay in wait for these men in the miles of steep, rocky road ahead.

Now may be a good time to take a look at the persons who are going to be with us on this trip.

Sam Hicks, something over six feet, slim, long-legged, long-armed, calmly competent, in the early forties, has been capable of coping with any emergency he has ever encountered during an adventure-filled life. He started out as a rancher, cowpuncher, bronco rider and trapper in Wyoming.

He and his father began outfitting hunting trips during the hunting season, as well as operating a string of ranches during the rest of the year. I first met Sam on an elk hunting trip and Sam is conceded, even by his competitors, to be just about the most skillful elk hunter in the State of Wyoming.

Sam came down to visit me and bit by bit a friendship developed until finally Sam let his ranching interests in Wyoming go and started working with me.

He is a great friend, a wonderful assistant. He is a good writer and on occasion writes articles which he sells under his own name to various magazines. He took quite a few of the photographs in this book. He is a skillful investigator and has worked with me on cases for the Court of Last Resort, knowing instinctively where to look for evidence, what evidence to look for, and can recognize evidence when he sees it.

He is a good all around outdoorsman, a wonderful shot, has a keen sense of humor, is always good-natured, and makes an ideal camping companion.

Murl Emery is a law unto himself.

49

Murl Emery, one of the greatest living authorities on Baja California, is a rugged, outdoor individual who spends more time in camp than home.

Murl went through a period when he wanted to be a businessman. He had a boating concession on Lake Mead where he would sell thousands of tickets every day; tickets ranging from seventy-five cents to twenty-five dollars, depending on the trip. He had a whole fleet of speedboats and a background of water knowledge which is encyclopedic.

Murl Emery was raised on the Colorado at a time when the river was a raging torrent of danger. He thought nothing of taking boats up and down the river, of shooting rapids, of living out in the arid desert while he was prospecting.

Then came the dams and the river was harnessed to a

succession of long, narrow lakes. Emery, having grown up with the river, naturally started in changing his environment with the river. However, there were business vicissitudes and, due to his involvement with others, Emery found himself going from riches to rags.

Emery went into mining and here he is superb.

Emery goes out and locates a mine just about whenever he wants to. He does this because he knows the desert intimately and because he is aware of the fact that most miners make their mistake in looking for metallic deposits of precious ores, whereas today much of the mining is in materials which the average man knows little about.

Beneath a rugged exterior of simulated indifference, Emery has one of the most probing minds I have ever met, remarkable powers of observation, a basic knowledge of geology, and a knowledge of how to live in camp that is surprising.

As Emery once expressed it to me, "Most people go on camping trips. I spend most of my life in camps."

And there are lots of things that a man must learn if he is going to camp.

It is nice to have a fine tent with a stove in it when one is camping. If the stove is properly designed it can be used for heating and cooking. But as campers have painfully learned, the stovepipe sucks up hot coals from the stove. These coals, under certain conditions, float briefly through the air, then settle on the tent, burning little holes the size of a pinhead, or, at times, setting the top of the tent afire, so that before the fire can be extinguished there is a great gaping hole with a perimeter of charred canvas.

Emery blithely takes a .22 revolver and shoots the stovepipe full of holes, then he builds his fire and forgets about the problem of a burning tent.

Why does this work?

51

Emery and Sam Hicks shoot the upper part of the stovepipe full of holes to avoid trouble with hot sparks burning holes in the tent.

I don't know. I assume that it somewhat lessens the velocity of the draft so that there is not enough suction to pull up burning embers from the stove beneath and I assume that once a burning ember does get in the stovepipe there is enough oxygen-laden air coming in from the outside so that the ember consumes itself before it spews out of the top of the stovepipe.

All I know is that it works.

I have camped in tents where we built fires and despite the fact we desperately tried to avoid burning the canvas, within a short time the tent was riddled as though it had been perforated with shot from a shotgun. I have even been in tents which caught fire and the burning roofs had to be extinguished with pails of water and then subsequently patched with pieces of canvas. But I have never had any fire trouble in one of Emery's tents or in one of Sam Hicks' tents and I know that they both shoot the stovepipe full of holes with a .22 six-shooter and then build roaring fires in the stove and forget all about the fire risk to the tent.

Murl Emery has one quality which has probably done more to bring about his success in mining than any other trait he has.

As he explained it to me at one time, the average miner is too much of an optimist. He gets a prospect, he has a good showing of gold, and he keeps on following this prospect. It doesn't get very much bigger but the miner has convinced himself there is a big vein just around the next bend, or back of the next few feet of rock. So he puts in all of his spare time and all of his money following this prospect.

Emery says every mine was once a prospect but that doesn't mean every prospect is destined to become a mine.

So Emery is completely hard-boiled about these things. He looks on a prospect with a professionally jaundiced eye. He refuses to waste his time and his operating capital on something unless he can prove it is good within a very limited period of time. Emery may have passed up a few fortunes in his life but he has certainly conserved his time and operating capital so that the mines he has developed are sure-fire and he feels, moreover, that he is able to go out in the desert and find a new mine just about any time he wants to.

Emery has something close to scorn for money and the responsibilities that go with it. He is a whimsical, outdoor, two-fisted philosopher, a very good mechanic, and a wonderful companion.

J. W. Black is a young man who is going places.

Black is something of a mechanical genius. He regards the world with the good-natured tolerance which is only found in people who are big enough and strong enough to know that they can lick any individual or anything that happens to get in their way.

I doubt if there is any mechanical problem Black can't

lick, and his strength is such that he can pick up pieces of iron I couldn't even budge, and handle them as though he were juggling confetti.

Black's mind is going all the time and what he sees he remembers and what he remembers he correlates.

Lee Sine, one of the other members on the trip, saw Black's Pak-Jak and he and his partner, Ray White, made Black a proposition to manufacture a consignment of them on a commercial basis. They took over the distribution and guaranteed to sell them at a minimum price.

It soon became apparent, however, that the problem was not going to be one of demand, but one of supply. Those first few machines which were manufactured were snapped up by the public and Black found himself forced to work nights, daytimes and on weekends in order even to begin to keep up with the demand.

Black, however, made one resolution: that after he had completed a specified number of these machines he was going to close the plant temporarily and take a trip somewhere, regardless of demand or pressures from the outside. He had remained firm in that determination and since Lee would have no machines to sell until Black got back into production, both men were able to take time off to accompany us to Baja California.

However, I doubt if wild horses could have kept them away from the trip; even if Black had been in production and Lee Sine had had machines running out of his ears, I think they would have somehow managed to come along on the trip.

Lee Sine is a man who does his own thinking, absorbs new experiences in silence, digests them thoughtfully, then reaches conclusions and is quite apt never to express an opinion until after his thoughts have been thoroughly crystallized into convictions.

Lee Sine.

It is readily apparent, therefore, that we had quite a group of individuals on this trip; a combination of men who had a knowledge of camping and of woodcraft, mechanical ability of a high order, versatility and ingenuity. One couldn't have asked for a better group in tackling a difficult assignment.

Since we had all agreed that the most feasible route was by water and making a landing at a point below which the whole network of canyons came together into a broad wash some four or five miles from the ocean, we were hoping for calm weather.

At this particular part of the coast, Angel de la Guarda Island, some fifty miles long, ends with high, rocky promontories veering at a sharp angle to the northeast.

Some fifteen miles away the shoreline of Baja California, with high mountains, angles sharply to the northwest. The result is that there is a wind trap which compresses the prevailing winter winds into a natural funnel; and this particular part of the gulf is apt to be rough when all the rest of it is smooth.

However, we felt certain that if we could only get breaks on the weather we could land our stuff on the beach, establish a base camp there and then have little trouble getting up into the canyons.

Of course it would be quite a job. We would have to get up the canyon far enough to find water, establish a spike camp there, then return to our base camp on the ocean, arrange to transport enough gasoline, food and sleeping bags to enable us to get by. Then we would move up from there a step at a time, making another assault on the canyon.

Both Munoz and Antero Diaz, however, had been skeptical about our ability to land our machines on the beach at the mouth of this wash. And a survey showed that if we landed them anywhere else we still had the problem of crossing mountains so steep and precipitous that they were almost straight up and down, and so strewn with huge boulders no wheeled vehicle could get over them.

However, the last days of December, 1960 were warm and balmy in Baja California and the gulf was flat calm.

We camped on New Year's Eve in a spot up in the granite country where we had previously camped on several occasions.

That granite country needs a word of explanation.

The peninsula of Baja California seems for the most part to be a mass of granite. In places the terrain has been worn and eroded until there is no soil visible — nothing but the granite and the sand of decomposed granite.

As one approaches the backbone of the peninsula the wind-worn granite takes on fantastic shapes. In places the rock has weathered and checked as the seams of softer material have weathered out, and great square boulders which look as though they must have been shaped by human hands, weighing thousands of tons, have either tumbled into confused piles or have balanced themselves precariously on some foundation which in turn has been worn away until it seems certain even a slight breath of wind must send the great boulders toppling down, leaving a path of roaring destruction in their wake.

There are also smaller boulders where the eroding effect of sand-laden winds have blasted away softer material, leaving the granite looking for all the world as though it were part of a man-made wall.

Elephant trees, those distinctive trees which are indigenous to Baja California and are found in only a few other similar places, seem to like the decomposed granite, and grow in profusion. There are also various other types of cacti and a species of greasewood growing here in the

Agaves, cardones and the weird cirio tree, which is found only in
Baja California and along a narrow strip on the mainland.

granite country. And just beyond it one encounters the
cirio tree, a tree which is found only in Baja California
and on the mainland near the gulf.

The cirio tree will at times grow perfectly straight, looking like a vast inverted parsnip, the butt end on the
ground, the point sticking some fifty feet into the air. It
will be covered with little stubby branches, six or eight
inches long, and these branches will have such foliage as
the tree produces. The whole effect is highly unusual.

However the cirio tree has certain peculiarities. At times
it will start bending over like an elephant's trunk after it
has attained a height of some twenty feet or so, and may
bend down until the tip touches the ground.

At other times the tree will grow straight until near
the top when it will suddenly branch out in a series of
five or six perpendicular terminals, stretching straight
toward the heavens.

Or the tree may bend and then send out terminal

branches, or again the tree may start to fork and one of the branches curl and twist as though in agony. All in all the cirio tree is highly individual and at all times highly distinctive.

Our first camp a few miles south of San Felipe had been hastily made as darkness approached, and was simply a place for a fire, a hurried sketchy meal and a night's sleep. But our second camp up in the granite country was one where we had a big campfire, where we brought out folding chairs and spent an hour or two of de luxe companionship.

It was New Year's Eve and we were mindful of that fact—not that we intended to sit up to see the New Year in.

Camping out in the open during the long winter nights inevitably changes one's sleeping habits.

At home I have difficulty sleeping more than three or four hours a night. I am usually working late at night and again early in the morning, and at times when I get really nervous I have the most irritating of all habits—that of being tired, going to bed, falling asleep, and then awakening with a start about two or three hours later, hopelessly wide awake and as stimulated as though I had been drinking a gallon of coffee.

Once I get out camping in the still, dry air of Baja California, however, the situation is different.

To begin with, any seasoned camper thoroughly detests cooking after dark. Emery always insists on making camp by four o'clock wherever possible so that the campfire can be made and the meal cooked before dark. Then the dishes are washed and put away and we sit around the campfire. We have a powerful radio and we are almost always able to bring in news from somewhere at six o'clock, with a weather forecast which may or may not be of value. Then we sit around to talk.

By six-thirty we are getting up and turning our backs to the fire for a while, to warm them up, then returning to the folding chairs for a few minutes, then again getting up and circulating around the fire.

By six-forty-five I usually decide that it would be a little more comfortable to crawl into my sleeping bag and listen to the conversation from the down-filled warmth of my bag and the soft cushion of an air mattress. The others decide to follow my example. Conversation continues for a few minutes, then like the campfire, begins to die down.

Some comment will come to my mind during a long period of silence. I will start to put the thought in words, then realize that after all it isn't quite worth the effort.

The next thing I know it will be midnight. The stars will be blazing steadily overhead, the campfire will have burned down to a few red coals gleaming fitfully through the ashes, and the outer atmosphere will be cold and silent.

Rounded rolls of white canvas, gleaming in the starlight against the darker ground, will mark the places where my companions are sleeping.

I will feel awake but not alert. I will roll over into the warmth of the sleeping bag, heave a deep sigh and look up at the stars for a while. I will be thoroughly convinced that having slept more than five hours already there will be no more sleep for me that night. So I will reconcile myself to remaining awake, watching the constellations.

I pick out the location of the various nebulae, marvel at the blazing brilliance of the stars in the crystal-clear silent atmosphere. I will settle myself into a slightly more comfortable position and then awaken to the realization that the east is a streak of color and that the stars have receded until only the brightest ones have become mere pinpoints which are rapidly fading into oblivion.

After a few nights one accepts the fact that normal bedtime is somewhere around six-thirty, and lets it go at that.

On one trip when we were interested in the news there was a very good broadcast that came on at seven-fifteen. Each night we made up our minds we would be up for that news broadcast. We never made it, but had to content ourselves with the six o'clock news the following morning.

In our complex civilization we are whipped into an artificial rapidity of pace which strains our nerves to the limit. But down in Baja California one suddenly sees things in a new perspective.

Those business deals which were so terribly important a few days ago are now relegated to the background. The tranquility of the silent, peaceful country is a soothing benediction to tense nerves. The calm satisfaction of having had a complete complement of sleep is, in itself, a soul-satisfying feeling. And while the campfire is made, breakfast cooked, the dishes washed and put away, the air mattresses deflated and the bedrolls tied, all with swift efficiency, there is no feeling of fighting the second hand of the watch. There is efficiency without haste.

One of the dividends of a trip by road down Baja California is the thrill of arising each morning with the knowledge that adventure is lurking somewhere ahead. It may or may not be just around the next bend in the road. Perhaps it is not within the next hundred miles. But somewhere along the road ahead one is certain there will be a real adventure and that each day will present problems which, while perhaps not dangerous enough and unexpected enough to be listed as real adventures, will nevertheless be something out of the ordinary requiring the exercise of a certain amount of ingenuity and on-the-spot thinking.

The trouble with civilization, or perhaps I should say one of the troubles with civilization, is that our lives are taken too much for granted. The very conveniences which we have invented to increase our efficiency, decrease our ability to cope with unexpected problems.

Our meals are cooked on electric stoves or gas ranges which have various automatic temperature controls; bread is converted into toast in an electric toaster which pops the slices out golden brown and piping hot when they have reached just the peak of perfection. The ice box enables us to reach in for milk and cream which has been kept perfectly fresh in handy-sized containers ready for pouring.

Every morning endless streams of humanity flow down to places where they take trains or busses. The busses in turn wend their way through congested traffic while the passengers are reading the morning paper, until finally all of these human ants have been converged into a vortex of seething activity at a time when a succession of carefully adjusted springs and cogwheels, turning minute and secondhands at a uniform rate, point to the hour of eight-thirty or nine o'clock as the case may be.

Here these human beings, by this time transformed into the component parts of some huge economic machine, are whisked upwards in elevators to the proper floor and arrive at offices which are heated by thermostatic control to exactly the right fraction of a degree making for human comfort.

All this is very nice, but there is something symbolic about it which is like the watch.

Each one of these individuals is wearing attached to his wrist one of these cogwheel devices actuated by a spring which moves minute and hour hands at a uniform rate so that at a given instant every one of these individuals sees the hands in exactly the same position as the hands which are attached to the watches on the wrists of all the other hurrying, jostling individuals converging toward the common center.

If the hands aren't uniform in their position, the owner hurries the watch to a jeweler who cleans, adjusts and fixes it so the man is once more in step with the remorseless march of time.

Down in Baja California you can throw your wristwatch away and you can throw your calendar away. You arise in the morning when it starts to get light. You gather the wood to build the fire. You let the fire die down to coals and on those coals you cook your breakfast. Your time guide for the day is the sun, and the shortening and lengthening of the shadows. Since the only purpose of a watch would be to tell you how much daylight was left in the day, it is easier to look at the shadows themselves than to estimate the time of sunset by consulting minute and hour hands. You are independent. You are on your own. Your activities are not coordinated with those of other people. There is, in short, no routine.

And always there is the knowledge that the day will be composed of interesting events, many of which will be completely unexpected.

I have taken many trips down the roads of Baja California and I have never yet taken one where something didn't happen that was worth while chronicling.

It is this feeling of having left the routine of civilization behind, of being on your own, of encountering each day as a challenge, that makes the exploration of Baja California roads such a delightful thrill. To have the benefit of a restful sleep in the open, to arise in fighting trim ready to meet the challenge of a new day—this is life!

While we had intended to wish each other a Happy New Year and perhaps have a New Year's drink the night before, sleep had stalked each one of us and caught us unaware. So we somewhat sheepishly wished each other a Happy New Year on January 1st, 1961, and having got the chores over and the camp loaded, were on our way a little after seven-thirty.

3

We Set out for the Palm-Lined Canyons

For the most part one can only make from eighty to a hundred miles a day in Baja California, if he is not driving himself to the point of fighting the road. And if he tries to fight the road and cover a few more miles the road is very apt to prove the victor in the conflict. In fact it is almost axiomatic in Baja California that haste not only makes waste, but makes complete destruction.

As Emery remarked from time to time during our stops, "Let's slow down so we can get there quicker."

After one has poked along at five to twelve miles an hour for several hours it is a welcome relief to come to the broad expanse of Dry Lake Chapala where, when the lake is dry, the soil is smooth as cement, and one can open the car up.

Even so, at such moments, shooting the car up to such breakneck speed that one feels positively reckless, he is apt to find on glancing at the speedometer that he is going perhaps forty-two miles an hour. In contrast to the pace he has been maintaining, this seems daredevil speed.

When, however, the lake is flooded, which it is at intervals during the winter season, and it becomes necessary to go around the lake, the experience is annoying in the extreme. The soil surrounding the lake is a silty combination of sand and loam. Every mud puddle in the road represents a bottomless trap which must be detoured. And the road itself is rutted almost hub deep. The slightest impatience is apt to result in a broken spring.

Arturo Grosso lives at Laguna Seca Chapala. He has not only a series of small typical ranch buildings but a well which gives good water.

It was only recently that Grosso was able to find water he could use. He could put down a well and get water all right but whenever he tried to irrigate a garden with that water everything curled up and died. There was something in it which killed vegetation.

On this occasion as we stopped to visit him, he was jubilant. He had secured water, he said, which was good water and which he felt certain would enable him to grow a garden.

Grosso is an intelligent man, an energetic man, and, according to Baja California standards, a rich man. He has many head of cattle and he has the ability to look and plan ahead. He has sufficient cash margin to hire cowboys and all through this section of the country Arturo Grosso is a power.

Grosso is friendly, speaks good English and is keenly interested in people and in events. He likes to chat for a few moments with travelers who pass by, but since he is a busy man with extensive interests it is usually difficult to find him when he isn't in the midst of some big undertaking such as rounding up cattle, shipping cattle or carrying on some ranching operation.

We stopped and paid our respects to Grosso, chatted with him for a few minutes, then moved on down the road.

We paused briefly at the ruins of the ghost city of Desengaño and then went on to Bahia de Los Angeles, arriving there about two o'clock on Sunday afternoon, just in time to be invited by Señor and Señora Diaz to participate in the fiesta.

It was quite a fiesta, with turtle soup and barbecued turtle.

The turtle—a big gulf turtle some three feet long—had been barbecued over mesquite-wood coals, by the simple expedient of cutting the turtle in two, propping the shells on rocks, building a fire in between and letting the meat along the inner shells cook to moist tenderness while the juices melted and ran down over the cooking meat. Then the meat is cut into cubes, the shell turned into a kettle and the meat allowed to simmer in the juice while peppers, garlic, lemon, onion and herbs are added.

We were in a spell of unusual calm and we were jubilantly anticipating being able to land without difficulty and establish a base camp.

But one doesn't do things hastily in Mexico and this is particularly true during the celebration of the New Year. Antero explained that he couldn't possibly get the boat ready before Tuesday morning at daylight, and in the light of subsequent developments it seems that getting things rounded up for Tuesday morning must have meant the application of quite a bit of pressure.

Antero said that we could load our things aboard the boat Monday afternoon and be prepared to start at daylight Tuesday morning.

So we settled ourselves to a period of relaxed waiting which, in my case, meant following the custom of the country by taking a siesta.

Sam, J. W. and Lee took Pak-Jaks and rode up a trail they discovered to an old mine high up on the mountain back of Bahia de Los Angeles. From this point of vantage they were able to get a breath-taking view of the entire bay. and they wanted me to go up there the next day with cameras and take some colored photographs.

However, after listening to their description of the trail, zigzagging in a series of hairpin turns up the side of a steep mountain, I decided to pass up the opportunity.

While a Pak-Jak "will go anywhere," it is no better than its rider and when it comes to negotiating the sharp hairpin turns of a steep trail with a canyon precipice on the down side, I am willing to do it if the necessity arises but I don't want to do it just for fun.

The Bahia de Los Angeles is wonderfully photogenic. It stretches in a great crescent with islands out in the gulf protecting the bay itself from most of the bad weather. The water is an intense blue, the sand a dazzling white, and the entire place is permeated with an atmosphere of friendliness.

The Mexicans who live there are dependent upon Antero Diaz for livelihood and Diaz is dependent for the most part on American tourists. The result is a friendly background of personal warmth which matches the balmy warmth of the climate.

Heaven alone knows how many people Antero can put up in a pinch. There are many cabins scattered around and the cabins have wide porches. When occasion requires, Antero can put up cots along these porches.

He never has the slightest idea of how many people are coming. A few people negotiate the road and come by car, but for the most part his patronage comes from air sportsmen who have discovered the place and realize that within a couple of hours' flying time from the border they can be in a fisherman's paradise where they can have marvelous food, accommodations with indoor plumbing, comfortable beds, and all at a cost that is absurd when compared with American prices.

The result is that on weekends plane after plane comes winging in from the United States and groups of excited tourists pull out fishing tackle, personal baggage and cameras.

Antero is on hand to greet them with genial hospitality, and assign them cabins. On Saturday night one is apt to hear excited voices in a veritable babble of conversation and the high-pitched sounds of feminine laughter until Antero brings about a curfew by stopping the Diesel motor which generates electric power.

On Sunday tourists are triumphantly holding up fish in front of cameras, guides are busy cutting filets from freshly caught fish and stacking them like cord wood.

Sunday afternoon one hears the roar of motors being warmed up. By Monday the place is back to normal with only those who have come in overland by automobiles and the passengers Francisco Munoz has brought in on his

Gardner and Dr. Carman inspect map of canyon country.

Dr. Carman takes us down for a closer look.

flights from Tijuana besides a few more or less permanent guests who have come to stay for one or two weeks.

Antero takes everything in his stride. Nothing fazes him. He always has his good-natured smile, his quick, energetic competence; there is always plenty of food, plenty of help and you are somehow given the feeling that while there may be other guests you are number one on the list.

It is little wonder that sportsmen everywhere talk about the charm of Bahia de Los Angeles.

Dr. Gordon Carman, a dentist of Beaumont, California, has made Bahia de Los Angeles almost a second residence.

Dr. Carman has leased some ground from Antero Diaz and has erected his own house. He has a plane and flies back and forth from time to time, virtually commuting between the place where he has his practice and the relaxing environment of Bahia de Los Angeles.

On Monday morning Dr. Carman dropped by to shake hands and suggested that since he wasn't leaving until noon it might be a good plan for us to make another survey of those canyons by air.

HOVERING OVER BAJA

Since Lee Sine had not seen the canyons from the air and since Murl Emery had been up enough to have a pretty good idea of the terrain, and because Carman's plane would hold no more than four passengers, it was decided that Sam, Lee, J. W. Black and I would accept Dr. Carman's generous offer and do a little more aerial exploration.

Lee Sine had flown in planes over the Himalayas during the war, so we assigned him the role of co-pilot and Sam and I took over the photographic assignment and we were off.

It was a beautiful day for aerial observation and Dr. Carman, a skillful flier, took us down into the canyons so that in places we seemed to be almost skimming the top of the palm trees.

Here were places within fifteen minutes' flight of the Bahia de Los Angeles where we could look down on a country where no tourist had ever been; perhaps where no human being had been for the last three hundred years.

From the plane we found grove after grove of interesting palms. We found long stretches of smooth canyon lined with palms on each side. We studied the whole labyrinth long

His curiosity aroused, Dr. Carman makes one very low swing over a canyon where no human being has been within modern times.

enough to realize that there were miles and miles and miles of country in which there would be novelty and adventure. Here we could see game as it existed in primitive surroundings. We were apt to find mountain lions and mountain sheep which had never had the slightest contact with a human being. While we were exploring we could bear in mind that no one knew what was just around the bend, because no one had ever been there and returned to tell the story.

We returned to the Bahia de Los Angeles, impatient to leave while the weather was still a flat calm.

There had been fiesta and celebration on New Year's Eve. We knew that there had been celebration the night before because we could hear the stringed instruments, the sound of soft Mexican voices singing from time to time during the night.

We had hardly anticipated that Monday night would also be a fiesta night but it was. All during the night when we wakened we could hear music and singing.

It seems that virtually everyone in Mexico can make music of sorts. They can strum a guitar and they can sing. And there is a softness, a plaintive something about the Mexican music which blends in with the temperament of the country and the velvety softness of the Mexican nights.

It was soothing to waken from time to time during the night and hear the sounds of the celebration—never the boisterous, raucous noises which emanate from an American celebration, but always the soft controlled cadences of melodious voices and a harmony of mind reflected in the tempo of the music and the type of singing.

All in all they made quite a band, with violin, guitar and a musical instrument which apparently took the place of our bass viol.

This consisted simply of a big inverted lard can with a hole punched in the top and a cord running through this hole and knotted on the end. The other end was tied around a broomstick to which the worn-out broom was still attached.

The musician would put the lower end of the broomstick near the perimeter of the tin can, then would tighten the cord by pulling back on the top of the broomstick. He would pluck at this cord and the result would be a deep percussive tone.

By tilting the top of the broom a little more and putting a little more tension on it, or relaxing it somewhat, this note could be changed noticeably and the instrument furnished a throbbing undertone causing the music to pulsate in hypnotic rhythm.

We wondered if our crew would be able to prop their eyes open with toothpicks so as to make the trip the next day, and I began to feel that the daylight start was simply a figure of speech.

However, we were up before daylight and Antero Diaz got up to turn on the Diesel motor so that we would have light. We got everything packed and all of our personal baggage ready to go and transported down to the edge of the ocean. Reassuringly, there were lights on the big boat indicating that it had started its generator and almost as soon as it was light enough to see, the crew came to get us in boats and take us aboard.

Once aboard, there were some delays in getting the motors warmed up and getting the anchor up, but within a reasonable length of time we were underway, creeping slowly out of the harbor.

It had been a beautiful night. The moon, very slightly past the full, had arisen to send a narrow ribbon of light over the bay. Then, as the moon got higher, the ribbon of light became broader until finally the whole bay was a silvery sheet of illumination, with the boats at anchor silhouetted in dark outline. Now, in the early morning, the moon was just setting over the mountains back of the settlement; it made a beautiful picture.

After we started crawling out of the harbor I took time to get acquainted with the two people Antero had selected to work with us on the trip: Ynes, who was to be something of a guide and general factotum, and to run the speedboat in case of necessity; and Juanito, who was to act as cook.

At the time I didn't appreciate the remarkable characters of these men. Juanito, quietly self-effacing, was a Tyrolean who had for some reason become a political refugee from Europe. He was a thoughtful man who spoke four languages (if one could count English), stooped with years and with much work, but quietly capable.

Ynes was essentially an adventurer and a hunter. Apparently, as we learned later, he was somewhere in his forties but he gave the impression of being much younger. He was powerfully built and, as I learned later, had about the keen-

Juanito in a characteristic gesture.

Ynes, instantly alert to the slightest motion.

est pair of eyes I have ever encountered. He had acute powers of observation, virtually no knowledge of English, and I think perhaps somewhere in the back of his make-up, a certain amount of scorn and perhaps pity, for the *gringo touristas* whom he must chaperone from time to time, and who were fat, soft and, according to his standards, enormously wealthy; and also according to his standards, completely helpless.

He carried his prize possession, a .30-30 rifle along with him, and it wasn't until an hour or so later that someone noticed a crude record had been scratched on the stock of the gun. The word *borregos* was preceded by six straight lines; then came *venados*, signifying deer, preceded by seven straight lines; then coyotes, preceded by six straight lines.

But we noticed there were some other scratches near the top of the stock and we twisted the gun so that when we finally got the light just right we could decipher what had been written there.

It was *Gringos,* preceded by two straight lines.

WE SET OUT FOR THE PALM-LINED CANYONS

This was to be the day of our great adventure. Our spirits were buoyed up enormously. We were on pins and needles, thrilled with excitement, impatient to get where we were going. The boat seemed barely to crawl along the gulf.

Juanito got down in the galley and cooked us breakfast: French fried potatoes, fried eggs, tortillas and coffee.

Then we were back on deck after breakfast, studying the shoreline with binoculars, talking in tense tones of suppressed excitement.

Our Pak-Jaks were tied along the chain which served as a rail for the boat. Our gear was safely stowed in the hold. We had a lot of provisions: apples, oranges, flour, bacon, canned goods, beans. We had gasoline, drinking water, cameras, films, sleeping bags, air mattresses, clothing.

We were loaded—so was the boat.

The first gusts of cold wind began to come in our faces and we bravely assured each other that this was just a mild sea breeze. Then the breeze began to freshen. Soon there were whitecaps and we then assured each other that this was just a local squall, that the weather was perhaps changing but that we would get up to our landing place early enough to take advantage of a relatively calm sea.

The wind freshened until it began to howl through the superstructure of the boat. Someone reported another boat

Our Pak-Jaks on the boat.

off on the starboard bow and we swung the binoculars around to see a shrimp fishing boat still farther out in the gulf making heavy weather of it while it came cruising shoreward on an angle which would intercept our course about three or four miles ahead.

Then suddenly while we watched, the boat abruptly changed course and headed directly for us. It came to within a few hundred yards, then veered off while the crew studied us intently, then forged on ahead. Apparently they had seen our deckload through binoculars and had wondered whether they were having nightmares or whether it was possible some boat, headed toward this trackless country where there was not even so much as a trail, would be carrying a deckload of motorcycles.

It soon became clear that this fishing boat was headed into a bay where a headland gave limited protection against the wind.

However, we were still brave and optimistic.

By the time we reached this bay, however, we were slapping spray up into the air as we hit the waves. The whitecaps were racing past, the wind was howling a gale, and it was obvious we were going to have to go into this bay and take advantage of what protection it had to offer.

Binoculars showed that several other fishing boats were also headed our way, indication of the fact that they all expected heavy weather.

Moreover, the barometer was falling rapidly.

We clawed into the best protection we could find and dropped the anchor but the force of the wind was such that we started dragging the anchor and had to keep the motors turning over in order to hold our position.

By this time several more of the shrimp boats were coming into the bay, dropping anchor and trying to hold against the wind. Most of them gave it up and, hoisting their anchor, went just as far into the bay as they dared to go and as close to the shore as they could get, dropping anchor in the area of maximum protection.

It was at this point that we all became weather experts.

Sam was positive the wind would go down about three o'clock that afternoon and it would be flat calm. He based his opinion upon what he had observed at the channel on prior trips.

Others hoped it would go down by two o'clock but we were all sure it would be flat calm by dark. The moon was full enough so that we could if necessary make a landing by moonlight.

That left us a day with nothing much to do.

So we started killing time and I think the crew took advantage of the situation to get caught up on some much needed sleep.

We soon found that by moving baggage around in the hold we could establish comfortable quarters there, spread out our sleeping bags and lie in relative comfort, protected from the wind.

I realized of course that if I slept during the day I wouldn't be sleeping at night but I couldn't resist the drowsiness of inactivity and from time to time would doze off in naps of an hour or so.

I had brought along two battery-powered dictating machines: the Audograph, which I had had with me on previous trips to Baja California and which had given me such good service; and one of the new Webcor Microcorders, a transistor-powered tape recorder which is remarkably sensitive and which is invaluable for a writer who wants to record conversations.

I used both of these machines as I dictated from time to time.

For the most part, however, I slept.

Then came the wind-blown night. The Diesel was stopped, the lights went out and we were left to our own devices in the hold of the boat, snuggled into our sleeping bags, the wind screaming overhead, the boat rocking in the waves.

Shortly after dark we had changed our anchorage, gone into the bay as far as we dared to go, and managed to get enough of a holding ground for the anchor so we could shut off the motors.

The boat was silent save for occasional creaking and the screaming wind. Our place in the hold was well ventilated through the open hatch but because of the tightly joined, insulated walls there was no suggestion of a draft.

We had all been sleeping and we all felt certain that we were going to be awake most of the night.

Much to our surprise, everyone had a perfect night's sleep.

I think there is quite a lesson here. We knew that there was nothing we could do if we were awake. We were in the only comfortable place on the boat; whatever was to come next would be the result of developments due to forces other than anything we could personally control. In fact there was nothing to do except sleep, so sleep we did.

Emery was the first one up the next morning. He poked his head through the hatch and exclaimed jubilantly, "We've got it made! The weather has changed. It's overcast. That means the wind is going to be from the south and during the period of change there'll be a flat calm."

All of us jumped up, dressed and waited impatiently for the crew to get up and in action.

What we didn't realize was that the crew had taken an earlier look at the situation, just at the first streaks of daylight, and not being quite as naïve nor quite as enthusiastic as Emery, had decided we were licked and gone back to bed.

Emery and Lee, their faces barometers of the second day of the storm.

Eventually the crew got up and Juanito started making coffee.

It should be mentioned at this point that we were in radio communication with Antero Diaz, who had a ship-to-shore radio installation, and who had telephoned us about nine-thirty the day before, apparently ready to suggest that we go back and try to get into the canyons over the mountains. In his opinion the water approach was going to be impossible for a rather extended period of time.

Sam, however, had been the one to talk with him and Sam, filled with optimism, had assured Antero the weather wasn't at all really bad where we were; that is, it was windy but it could be a lot worse.

Antero reported that the bay was calm but binoculars showed him that the gulf out beyond the islands was whipped into a turmoil of raging whitecaps. Quite apparently he had wanted us to turn back but Sam had pooh-

poohed him for being chicken-hearted. We were going to the canyons or bust and we weren't going to get there by turning back.

When the wind began to come up this next morning all of us felt pretty discouraged. The crew got up, took a look, and it was possible to see from their facial expressions what they felt the weather was going to be. We didn't need an interpreter or a Spanish-English dictionary.

And the faces of Lee Sine and Murl Emery were pretty darn good barometers of skepticism. As they sat huddled in the lee of the cabin, I couldn't resist snapping a photograph which was even more eloquent than words.

By nine-thirty Antero Diaz was on the phone again. This time I insisted that as time was dribbling through our fingers, we yield to his superior judgment. He thought we had better go back to Bahia de Los Angeles and try to get over the mountains. He felt certain the weather was going to be rough for some days.

It was not a popular decision but we made it. We got the anchor hoisted and started back with a tailwind pushing us on, and arrived shortly before noon.

Antero Diaz was all apologies. In true Mexican fashion he wished to assume all the blame. The cursed weather had betrayed him, but he couldn't refrain from pointing out that we must expect wind this time of the year. He had warned us. "No?"

We reminded him there had just been four or five days of clear calm and Diaz nodded vehemently. It was too bad. We had just missed it. If we had only been a day earlier perhaps. He eloquently shrugged his shoulders. But he felt certain we could get in through the dry lakes. After all, there was only one little hump to get the machines over and he was certain we could do it.

That, however, brought up another problem. We certainly couldn't get any trailers over those mountains and we couldn't carry enough on the Pak-Jaks to establish a base camp in the canyons if we ever got there. So we were going to have to get a string of mules that could pick their way into the canyon somehow.

Antero was certain that a mule could go wherever the Pak-Jak could go.

J. W. wasn't quite so certain.

But it was finally arranged that Antero would locate Pepe Smith, who had a string of mules and burros. Smith and Sam would round up all the mules and burros on the ranch, and Pepe would take off, prepared to join us somewhere at the head of the dry lake.

I wanted to arrange a definite rendezvous and Antero smiled tolerantly. We didn't need to worry. Pepe would find us. Wherever we were, that was where Pepe would come with the mules and burros.

Since Pepe was going to have to go some forty miles, we started him getting his stuff together and then took a quick trip with the cars and the Pak-Jaks down to the ghost town of Las Flores.

Putting our Pak-Jaks to work while loading and unloading our gear.

Left to right: Gardner, Lee Sine and J. W. Black at the ghost town of Los Flores.

Seventy years ago Las Flores was a flourishing mining community with great prosperity and great hopes. The promoters had even shipped in a locomotive and put up a narrow-gauge railroad line, running from the mine to the town where the mill was to be located.

For some years the mine had been in production and then it had closed down. Now the buildings were in ruins, the rusty locomotive had been partially dismantled, and the tracks had been left to rust to pieces.

Using our Pak-Jaks to help us cover distance we made quite an exploration of the town and of the surrounding terrain.

We found the graveyard which had been the last resting place of the aristocracy. It had been surrounded by a fence of handcarved hardwood. Now the posts had fallen down and years of fierce sunlight had drained the moisture from the wood causing deep cracks or checks.

The wealthy people had been buried in one graveyard, the peons in another; a class distinction which apparently was supposed to endure after death.

Now that the town is dead, the town and the two grave-yards are all blended together in that tranquility which is a part of the ageless dignity of death. Not only were all distinctions abolished but the community which had made the distinctions was abolished.

While most of the town was still standing in roofless ruin, the jail, having been constructed of masonry so as to offer a more secure place to house law violators, remains virtually as it was seventy or eighty years ago.

It is interesting to note that at various places in the rock walls of this jail there are deep scratches, made painfully and laboriously with a nail, indicating where some unhappy prisoner of half a cenutry ago had marked the passage of time. It is also interesting to reflect that the monument to wrongdoing should be so much more permanent than the other structures.

We inspected the old rusted locomotive, and then, using our Pak-Jaks, prowled around the site of the village, picking up little discarded bits of evidence of a bygone civilization.

Emery inspects the old jail at Los Flores.

#4

Where No Human Foot Has Trod

The next day we were off for the dry lakes.

We had a great assortment of Pak-Jaks, tents, water, gasoline, sleeping bags, provisions and cameras.

Ynes and Juanito were riding on top of the load, and since they were the official guides it became necessary from time to time to have conferences with them. So we would stop the car and Sam would climb up one side, I would climb up the other, and we would have a series of conferences.

We crossed the first dry lake, plowed along in four-wheel drive into the rough country on the other side of the lake and began to see wild burros.

Whereas the tame burro moves along in calm patience, apparently only mildly interested in whatever new vicissitude of fortune life has in store for him, these wild burros hold their heads high and are proud of their freedom. They swish their tails in nervous indignation at the approach of a vehicle and then take off across the desert in that peculiar half-trot, half-gallop which is characteristic of the species, and which can cover ground at an astonishing rate of speed.

The wild burro is esteemed as remarkably good eating by everyone who has tried it, and while I think perhaps I have eaten wild burro on occasion without knowing it, I have always tried to discourage the killing of wild burros.

I had two pet burros once who gave me their confidence, and in turn received my confidence. We had a wonderful companionship. Moreover, I learned a great deal.

The burro can understand just about everything he wants to and he is adept at pretending not to understand the things he doesn't want to understand, but which you want him to. He can look at you with patient lack of comprehension yet at the same time not only know what you are saying to him, what you want, but what you are going to say and what you are going to want, and exactly what he intends to do about it.

And heaven help the human being who pits his restless impatience against the mind of a burro.

On some of the old-time cattle ranches where there was a great distance between headquarters and the outlying grazing country, when they found a steer that was too "snaky" to drive in a herd and would break away at the first opportunity and head into the brush, they had one cure which always worked.

They would drive a burro from ranch headquarters out to the brush. They would corner the steer, rope him and then tie him firmly to the burro. Then they would go away.

In the course of time the burro would show up at the ranch with a steer that weighed five times as much as he did.

From the viewpoint of the burro there was nothing to it. When the steer would start moving away from the ranch he would have to drag the burro. Whenever the steer would

Wild burros show the unmistakable stamp of freedom.

move toward the ranch the burro would move under his own power. At first the steer would drag the burro wherever he wanted to go, but eventually the pair would show up at the ranch.

Such is the power of patience.

Never underestimate the burro.

Juanito had prospected over much country and had a general idea of the lay of the land. Ynes had hunted over much of the country and knew a good deal about it. Sam, J. W. Black, Lee Sine and I had flown over the country looking for landmarks and getting the country "firmly fixed" in our minds. Sam insisted he could pick out landmarks on the ground that he had seen and noted from the air.

As far as I was concerned, I had carefully studied the terrain, and I was lost. Looking at the country from the air was one thing and looking at it from the ground was another. However, when it comes to argument I'm damned if I'm going to be left out of an argument simply because I don't know what I'm talking about.

So we drove and argued and argued and drove, and eventually came to a spot where we pitched our tent in the very late afternoon of an overcast day.

That night I awakened to look at the moonlight.

It was a cold, windy night and the shadows were coming from the wrong direction. Incredulously I took another look. The camp was facing in the exact opposite direction from what I had thought it was the night before; either that, or else the moon was coming up in the wrong direction.

In the morning we had an argument as to directions and Sam impatiently traced a cross on the floor of the tent, marking north, south, east and west. When the sun came up it came up in the west as far as I was concerned, and to the south as far as Sam's diagram was concerned. In fact everyone was turned around and I am inclined to think that that is one day that the sun got tired of coming up in the same old direction day after day and decided to have a little variety.

We had a hurried breakfast, then Sam, Emery, Lee Sine, J. W. Black and Ynes all swarmed aboard the pickup which contained the Pak-Jaks and started exploring the country, headed toward a mountain which Sam swore he could recognize from his airplane observations.

In view of the fact that he hadn't known where the sun was coming up I was inclined to take this with what is known as a pinch of salt and a barrel of pepper.

I decided to stay in camp with Juanito and we had a leisurely visit together during which Juanito gave me much of his history. He never talked about the Old Country or what had happened there, but by using sign language, English and fragmentary Spanish, I gathered that Juanito had spent some two years shark fishing, making his headquarters at a spring known as La Botica, which was near the wash which we had wanted to explore by boat, and where we wanted to make our base camp. We had heard from others that there was a spring near there and that fishing boats sometimes put in to replenish their store of drinking water.

Juanito had also had some interest in a ranch which was back near the site of the old mission of Calamajue. He had from time to time walked back and forth from his camp on the beach to this ranch and in doing so had traversed one of the canyons. I gathered it was the most northerly canyon of the system we wanted to explore. He said no one else had ever been there.

Juanito said there was a spring of water about twelve miles from the ocean and about thirteen or fourteen miles from the ranch. He would make the trip in two days, trudging through the long, hot, sandy canyon, until he reached this water; staying there at night, then getting up the next morning and then moving on down to his camp.

This had been seventeen years ago when one gathered that Juanito had pushed himself to the limit, walking as rapidly as possible so that he could leave the ranch in the afternoon and get to the spring, then leave the spring early in the morning and get down to his camp in time to go to work shark fishing.

Juanito was now seventy-one. He was stooped somewhat and he had lost many of his teeth, most of which he had apparently been forced to extract by himself. He was now having another toothache and intimated he would probably have to extract another tooth in the near future.

But there was no complaint in Juanito's nature. He was like a burro. He took things as they came and he wasted no time in wishing that they might be otherwise.

As I came to know him later, here was a man in his seventies, who could ride all day on a burro after cooking breakfast and helping to pack the burros, who could come into camp at night bone tired yet quite ready to get out the pans and start cooking over the fire, then in the light of the campfire, clean up the dishes and get everything put away shipshape before going to bed.

It is something of a job riding a burro hour after hour in the sun, particularly if a man is heavy and Juanito was carrying a good deal of weight.

Ynes, the hunter, stocky build, thick-chested, with short arms and legs, was a walker. He wasn't built to walk but he walked anyway.

Now, Sam Hicks is a natural walker. He has long legs, a slim waist and lean flanks. He devours the distance with long, easy strides.

Ynes, on the other hand, being short-legged took a step and a half to Sam's one, but he used those short legs of his like powerful pistons. As I got to know the man better I was surprised to find the extent of his endurance. He would stand up to a day which would leave the ordinary man as limp as a dishrag. He would cover ground which even a good walker would have considered a long day's work, and then he would be ready to pitch in and go to work when we were making camp.

Shortly after noon Emery came back filled with excitement. They had explored the mountains and decided we couldn't get over them. Then, just as they were about to give up, Lee Sine had found an old, old trail.

This trail apparently went back to the time of the missions. Along the sidehill many of the huge boulders had rolled down in the last hundred years or so until the trail was in places virtually obliterated. But farther on one would come to places where the trail was again fairly open. And up on the mesa above the first mountain ridge the trail was in good shape.

By working on this trail and moving the rocks that could be moved where they blocked the trail, and for the rest relying on the rugged hill-climbing ability of the

It is easy to see the trail on the top of the mesa, but on the sides of the mountain it had been choked with a century of rolling rocks.

Pak-Jaks, Sam, Black and Sine were trying to move the machines up the hill.

Ynes had started back earlier before they had found this trail and had said that he would be in camp at two-thirty. As soon as he arrived we were to move the entire camp to a point near the start of the trail.

Since Ynes carried no watch and the route he was going to take was a long, arduous walk along the ridge of mountains, I was somewhat apprehensive that he would be late. He was going to have to tell time by the sun.

I could have spared myself the worry. Ynes showed up in camp at exactly two-twenty-eight.

Moving the camp was some little chore. But Ynes and Juanito tackled the job with skilled efficiency. Emery furnished both manpower and direction and within a surprisingly short period of time we had the camp loaded and started out, following the tracks in the deep sand, getting up to our new camping place shortly before dark and pitching the tent — again in a cold wind.

Sam, Black and Sine came back down the trail, three

tired men. But they had moved the four Pak-Jaks which they had with them up to the top of the mountain. (My Pak-Jak had been left behind in camp in case I wanted to do some exploring on it. Otherwise they would have had it with them.)

So while everyone was tired that night, they felt that they had the hardest part of the job behind them and that they were going to be able to get the Pak-Jaks down into the wash early the next day so we could start out.

Sam insisted that this was the wash which led down to the other wash by the ocean and eventually, by using it, we could reach the canyon we wanted to explore. He pointed out landmarks he had seen from the air.

These were also landmarks I had seen from the air.

They didn't look like anything I had ever seen before.

We started fixing up light packs of bare essentials. Pepe Smith would bring eight mules and burros. That would leave four burros for packing because we had to have riding burros for Smith, his twelve-year-old son Nenny, and for Juanito and Ynes; although Ynes insisted that he would be able to walk right along and keep up with the burros.

It is interesting to note parenthetically that on this trip Ynes did so much walking he literally wore a pair of shoes to shreds. By the time the trip was over the soles were flapping loose from the uppers. I am reminded under such circumstances of a remark made by Bill Sullivan, an Idaho outfitter who has taken me on several trips into the primitive area. "My shoes were so damned thin," Sullivan was wont to state, "that whenever I'd go to town and step on a piece of chewing gum I could tell what flavor it was."

Early in the morning Sam, Lee Sine and Ynes started up the hill to move the Pak-Jaks down to the flat on the other side. J. W. Black took my Pak-Jak to "ride" up to the top of the hill.

Pepe Smith ran the mule train assisted by his twelve-year-old son "Nenny," who did a man's work.

"Riding" these Pak-Jaks over obstructions such as huge boulders calls for much skill and, at times, considerable strength.

The rear wheel of the Pak-Jak is going to keep revolving. You can put the front wheel up against a building and the rear wheel will keep revolving slowly and steadily until it has dug a hole or worn all the tread off the tire.

When one comes to an obstruction in the trail one is supposed to put his feet down on the ground, give a gentle push and open the throttle slightly. The Pak-Jak leaps forward and up, and then you either drop on the seat as it goes by or partially close the throttle, take another step and give another little burst of power. At times you have to reach back and pick up the rear frame of the Pak-Jak and literally lift it over some obstacle which is so spaced that the frame of the Pak-Jak gets "hung-up."

However, given a big rear wheel which is going to

keep revolving no matter what happens, it is surprising what one of those things can do.

The terrifying thing, however, is when one loses his footing or perhaps gets a foot tangled in a rock and the Pak-Jak, with that steady, remorseless power, keeps right on going. Even if you are only moving at the rate of a mile and a half an hour that can seem to be a terrific speed under some circumstances. It's difficult to coordinate one's reactions fast enough to synchronize wheel, throttle and brakes and keep up with what is happening — I know because I've been there and have the scars to prove it.

Pepe Smith showed up with the mules and burros a little after nine o'clock. Don't ask me how he had found us. He knew where we were and came unerringly to the place where we were camped. Not to the place where we had been camped the day before, but to the place where we were camped now.

Smith is a tall, taciturn individual who has known his share of tragedy. He had a large family and then recently his wife died, leaving him with all the children and the necessity of making a living as well as keeping the home together.

Pepe was accompanied by his twelve-year old son Nenny, an alert, intelligent lad who was as full of bounce as a rubber ball. That boy did a man's work all during the trip. He rode from daylight to dark, he helped pack burros, he would hobble the burros at night, had sufficient skill to track each individual burro the following morning, knew how to saddle pack and unpack, and always tackled every task — not with the attitude of trying to do a chore — but with enthusiasm and endless energy.

Looking at him one could only wonder at the responsibilities he had had to take on, both at home and out in the field; remembering that there were seven children, and that five of them were younger than he was, one could realize something of the situation and appreciate more fully what it meant to have a young man so competent, so cheerful, and above all so quick to get into action and accomplish what he was called on to accomplish.

Even traveling light we had our pack burros pretty badly overloaded. One burro in particular had to carry two five-gallon cans of water, two five-gallon cans of gasoline and a bag containing other equipment. Figuring water at eight pounds to the gallon and the cans weighing three or four apiece, that burro was carrying well over two hundred pounds. And he was carrying it over country that was rough, steep and rugged; then down into soft sand where a man's feet would sink with every step. The poor little burros, carrying this amount of weight, sank several inches every time they put down a hoof.

We left all of our surplus supplies in the tent; most of our cameras, the dictating machines, films, provisions, drinking water, gasoline and some of our bedding.

The tired pack train, with over-loaded burros, wearily plods along— perhaps the only burros ever to enter this canyon.

I started out about ten-thirty to walk up the trail and over the mesa to where the Pak-Jaks would be waiting on the other side.

It was a long, tough climb just pushing my way up and it was more than two hours later that I got down to where I could see where Black and Sine had the other Pak-Jaks waiting.

It turned out to be quite a job getting the mules and burros over the mountain, even with the trail which the men had cleaned out as much as possible. Once one of the burros got all tangled up in the rocks and was smart enough to know that he couldn't dislodge himself without breaking a leg, so he simply stayed put until everything had been unpacked and rocks had been moved and he had been lifted to his feet. Then he was repacked and consented to move on.

At length, however, we had the whole expedition together at the start of a broad wash leading in the general direction we felt we wanted to go, and started off.

The burro fails to negotiate the rocky slope. Left to right: Pepe Smith, Nenny, Juanito.

We on the Pak-Jaks were so impatient that we would cruise far ahead of the burros and then either wait for them to catch up or double back to make certain everything was coming all right.

It was a wonderful thrill going down that wash. Not only was the scenery beautiful but we had the knowledge that within the last twenty or twenty-five years no one had been in that wash. Pepe Smith, Juanito and Ynes were the men who would have been there if anyone had been, yet none of them had ever set foot in this country. Pepe Smith hadn't known about the ancient trail we had uncovered and was very pleased to have learned of it.

In short, we were exploring brand-new country.

After two or three miles the wash broadened out into a sort of amphitheater with granite cliffs closing in on three sides and a gentle up-slope on the other. It looked very much as though we were hemmed in but we realized that in times past, during periods of storm, quite a bit of water must have run down this wash and it had either found some outlet or would have formed a lake, and there were no signs of a lake. So we kept on going.

Abruptly the wash turned into a canyon between granite cliffs, but the floor remained sandy and it was easy to keep going with Pak-Jaks.

After several miles of this it began to get late in the afternoon and I felt we should make camp where there would be feed for the mules and burros.

These hardy little creatures feed on mesquite, or if there is a verde tree available and a few limbs can be chopped down, they will browse on these leaves and seem to get along all right.

It was destined to be a dry camp for the animals and I understood the preceding night had also been a dry camp. It is remarkable what these mules and burros can do in dry country, particularly if they are not worked too hard or encounter too much hot weather.

Pepe Smith was, however, anxious to press on just as far as possible before dark, so he suggested we move on for another half hour.

The burro which was overloaded — the one carrying the water and gasoline — knew somehow that I was looking for a campsite and that my voice indicated I was sympathetic.

That burro started following me around like a dog. If I would get away from the main wash, where I could investigate what I thought might make a good place to camp and would sit there waiting for Pepe to come up, that burro would spot me and come up to me, then turn and stand so that his left side was to me and all but thrust the knot of the pack rope into my hands.

At length, just as the canyon was bathed in a deep pool of shadow, the riders who had been on ahead came back with alarming news.

They had reached a place where there was a sheer drop of forty or fifty feet. During periods of flood there must have been quite a waterfall there. In the meantime the bed of the canyon simply came to a steep rocky barrier, dropped fifty feet and then resumed its way toward the sea.

This was disturbing news indeed. It looked as though we might have to turn, retrace our steps, fight our way back over the mountain and give up all hope of ever getting into the palm-lined canyons.

We ate a rather gloomy supper although Sam was confident that we were within a few miles of the place where the canyon merged into the wash we wanted to follow.

I suggested that Sam try to scale one of the canyon walls so that he could get to the top and see if he could

Left to right: Pepe Smith, Juanito and Ynes unloading for camp.

spot the ocean and see how far away it was. But Ynes, who had been looking around, motioned to Sam and they vanished into the late afternoon shadows.

I learned afterwards that they climbed down the rock wall, walked about half a mile and then came to a place that Ynes knew — a place he had found in his walk up from the ocean on a previous trip. With that landmark once established Ynes knew the whole country.

So just before it got good and dark, Sam and Ynes were back with the encouraging news that we could probably get up to the palm canyons if we could only find some way of getting our Pak-Jaks down the face of that cliff.

Nevertheless I was worried. We might use ropes to lower our equipment down that cliff, but could we ever get back up. We had food and water for a very brief trip. I could never have walked back to base camp.

I didn't do much sleeping, yet I will long remember the beauty of that night.

This air, despite the fact it is near the ocean, was free of humidity and clear as crystal. I could look up and see the stars in great profusion. The Milky Way was a silvery star stream, and I could pick out individual stars which could never be seen at all in the more polluted atmosphere around the cities.

I slept and then wakened as the slightly lopsided moon came up over the canyon wall.

There were smoke trees in the canyon. Having a light, silvery blue shade and lacy, spine-like leaves, they look for all the world like drifting smoke. As the moon came over the rim of the canyon the mountain was a silhouetted black of intense shadow. The wash turned to brilliant silver and these smoke trees, outlined against the black of the shadow, were turned by the magic of moonlight into silvery clusters.

Over all was the blanket of absolute, complete silence. I knew that the following day would hold adventures — many adventures.

I dozed off and slept soundly until the first streaks of daylight, when we were up and getting camp organized.

By broad daylight we went down to take a look at the face of the cliff.

Some of the others could negotiate that cliff by lowering themselves down on the waterworn rocks, then angling along through a fissure and then finally moving slowly down a steep ledge only a few inches wide with a straight drop at the back of it and only a precarious handhold.

I might have done it, I don't know. And I might have been seriously injured. I had to have help to get down there and I didn't make any bones about it.

Right now the problem was whether we could ever get our camp equipment and our Pak-Jaks down this ledge. If we could, we had it made. If we couldn't, we were licked.

Pepe Smith surveyed the surrounding country, and finally found a route by which he felt he could get the burros up onto the wall of the canyon, inch his way around to a point below the barrier, then descend down to the lower canyon and lead the mules back up to the rocky wall.

We in turn could roll all of the camp stuff into bundles and lower it with ropes over the face of the cliff.

The Pak-Jaks, however, presented quite a problem. They weigh around a hundred and seventy-five pounds apiece and they have two wheels and are precariously balanced. If we could find some way of keeping them upright so we could use the wheels to ease the load we felt we could make it, but they would have to be kept upright and everything would have to work like a charm.

So we got all the rope we could and started working our vehicles down the cliff a few inches at a time, holding them snubbed with a rope, letting them roll for a few inches, then straightening them; letting them roll for a few more inches until finally we came to the last fifteen or twenty feet which was a sheer, absolute drop. There was nothing we could do except snub a rope and trust to luck.

It was touch and go for a while but we finally got the first Pak-Jak lowered down to the floor of the canyon below and after that the others came faster. Whether we could ever get them back up was another question — one that gave me increasing concern.

We didn't wait for Pepe Smith to get the burros all back and loaded but, impatient as we were to see what lay ahead, started the Pak-Jaks and moved on down the canyon.

A mile or so on down the canyon Ynes indicated we were to take a canyon which went to the left. We did so and came to the unmistakable indication of water. There was a yellowish type of coarse grass up ahead, completely covering the canyon. And there were bones. Heaven

Lowering Pak-Jaks down rocky cliff. Left to right: Lee Sine and Sam Hicks. Below, J. W. Black.

knows how many bones there were. These were the skeletons of mountain sheep and they were there by the dozen.

There were indications that this canyon had been used by the Indians as a hunting ground. There were typical Indian hunting blinds, so constructed that hunters could shoot a bow and arrow through openings so placed that the game must pass within fifteen to twenty-five feet of them.

We found a pile of bones which could have been covered by a good-sized blanket and in that one pile we counted the remains of thirty different sheep.

Some of these undoubtedly had been killed by mountain lions — we saw many lion tracks — some few probably by bullets and perhaps some by Indian arrows. And it was possible some of these had died of old age.

Ynes insisted that when the mountain sheep became too old to forage in the hills they came down to this spring to live out their old age, and finally to die.

The bones would certainly so indicate.

The bones of thirty mountain sheep in an area one could cover with a large tarp.

Native hunters could hardly have accounted for these skeletons, nor for the very good heads of horns which were lying there in the sunlight — although we had now reached a point so near the ocean it was possible some hunters had found this spring.

We tasted the water at the spring. It seemed to be strongly flavored with soda, just as though a person had put a teaspoonful of baking soda in a glass of water.

I have a feeling that it would have been possible to have found many arrow points here in this canyon. Undoubtedly the Indians had rigged up blinds almost from time immemorial and had ambushed the mountain sheep as they came to drink. Some day I hope to return and make a search for arrow points and again study this canyon, but at the moment we had no time for that. We were determined to get to the canyon of the palms, go up past the first few intersections and see just what the situation looked like from the ground.

We got on our Pak-Jaks and started on down the canyon which speedily widened into a wash with towering cliffs of pastel pink, orange and a bluish green.

The pink seemed to predominate and there were whole mountains of vivid pink; some sort of a colored compressed volcanic ash. We didn't climb up to see exactly what materials composed these various strata. In fact the sides were virtually sheer in places. However I did inspect some of the cliffs where the coloration came down to the floor of the wash.

The material seemed to be a compressed ash, colored a delicate, uniform pink with no streaks in it at all.

This formation ran for miles along the coast, cropping out here and there in various places.

As we descended toward the ocean the wash became wider and wider until finally we reached its intersection with another wash and saw an outcropping of this pink

We ride rapidly up a canyon which has never before known North Americans.

formation thrust up out of the canyon floor right at the junction of the washes.

We knew now that we were on the right track, since we had previously spotted this same pink outcropping from the air and knew that it marked the place where the palm canyon wash joined the others.

So we waited for the mules and burros to catch up to be sure we were all headed up the right canyon, then turned and started up this other wash.

Within a half a mile or so we began to realize that this canyon must have lots of palm trees in it. There were evidences of floods and the trunks of palm trees were scattered around like match sticks.

It is difficult to account for these floods. They must have been within modern times. Yet it is a land of little rainfall. However, occasionally during the summer months a

104

chubasco or Mexican hurricane comes roaring up the gulf. At those times there is a tremendous amount of rainfall and there are many indications that because of local conditions these canyons and the surrounding country get rainfall when the rest of the peninsula is bone-dry.

We pressed on hurriedly now, eager to get up into the clusters of palms we had seen from the air. The sun was intense and looking down at the reflected sunlight from the white sand was agonizing. Yet I put off wearing dark glasses because I find that these ruin my sense of exposure in photography.

As we worked our way up the wash the mountains on each side began to press together until we had the beginning of a wide canyon looming ahead of us. And here we began to encounter rough going in places. There would be spots of a few hundred yards where the sand had been washed away, leaving rocks piled in confusion which we had to fight our Pak-Jaks over.

We pressed on for what seemed to me to be an interminable distance and found the mountains coming closer together until we were very definitely in another canyon.

Then along in the afternoon we saw our first palm — a stately tree standing in solitary splendor.

Just before we came to this palm, however, there was a branch in the canyon and our airplane explorations had indicated that we should take this right-hand branch because it seemed there was a veritable oasis, with water, some few miles up the right-hand canyon. Morover, Juanito had said this was the canyon which had the good spring — "Agua Buena."

So while we went up a half mile or so to look at the lone palm tree, Pepe Smith with the mules and burros went on up the right-hand canyon.

The chips were down now and we were gambling for

keeps. This was the third day the mules and burros had been without water and they simply had to have water that night. If they didn't get it, they couldn't get back out of the canyons and if they couldn't get out of the canyons, we couldn't, because the burros were carrying gasoline for the Pak-Jaks, as well as drinking water for us.

We had seen what seemed to be an oasis from the air up this right-hand canyon and Juanito had told us of the spring that had been there seventeen years ago, but springs have a habit of drying up and there was always the possibility that Juanito could have been mistaken.

It is an uncomfortable feeling when one realizes that he has left the comforts of civilization so far behind that his very life is dependent upon some little thing. Junanito was well past seventy. It was quite possible that his memory had begun to play tricks on him. We were staking our lives on the accuracy of his memory and on the fact that a spring which had existed seventeen years ago would still be in existence today.

As the heat of the canyon gradually dehydrated our tissues, as I began to realize more and more the importance of reaching water sometime that afternoon, I began to take stock of the situation. Or as Emery expressed it, take a good, long look at my hole card.

So we paused only briefly at the lone palm tree, then turned, retraced our steps and started going up the right-hand canyon.

Here we again encountered a little rough going for a spell, then came a smooth stretch, and then we came to four large palm trees where we stopped for photographs and a little well-earned rest in the cool shade.

However, since we could see the glistening fronds of other palm trees up the canyon, we cut short our rest. As we went up the canyon, cluster after cluster of palm trees appeared and the shade became more and more welcome.

We were also encountering tougher going, with places where the water had formed riffles as it fell rapidly during periods of flood and had left great barriers of water-worn rocks.

These were not too serious an obstacle but we realized that excitement and a very, very strenuous day, following a whole series of strenuous days, had brought about a certain amount of emotional fatigue as well as just plain physical weariness.

We had had too many experiences crowded into too short a time.

As we pressed onward the canyon narrowed and again we found more palms. I kept thinking that each cluster of palms we were approaching must be the place where we had seen the oasis from the air. It seemed that we must have gone past our destination.

However, Sam and Ynes were on ahead — Sam had fixed up an improvised seat on the back of his Pak-Jak and

We make camp and relax.

they were riding double. We knew that Sam and Ynes would have turned back if there had been any serious trouble and felt that they were probably resting by a spring of cool water.

Such is the process of the human mind, that as we encountered more and more palms in the canyon we began to take them for granted.

I was hungry, thirsty, and too dog-tired to appreciate the marvelous scenery.

Finally after fighting across a rocky bar and coming to a level stretch, suddenly we saw ahead such a tremendous growth of palms that we knew it must be the oasis.

Sure enough, we found Sam and Ynes waiting for us, the mules and burros hobbled, and good old Juanito, despite the long strenuous day, busying himself with cooking.

We had the luxury of a wash, then a long cooling drink. Then I settled down in the shade to rest.

Despite the fact that I was physically tired, I got up in a short while and started looking around. I couldn't rest, and I know the others felt the same way.

Here we were in virgin country and we might find anything around the next bend in the canyon.

Ynes decided he would take a walk and Lee Sine went with him.

I watched them go, wishing I had the energy to join them; but knowing that Ynes' short legs were going to be pounding up that canyon and that Lee Sine, an expert hiker and deer hunter, was going to be hard put to keep up with him, I sat down again.

I dozed for half an hour, then awakened to watch the long shadows in the canyon and suddenly knew that I simply had to take a walk.

So I told the others I wouldn't be going far, would keep in the canyon and would be careful not to get into any trouble.

Gardner in Sal Si Puede Canyon.

In most of the country where I have traveled with Pak-Jaks, game has become accustomed to the sound of gasoline motors. There are enough through highways, enough automobile traffic, so that wild game has come to take motor noise more or less as a matter of course. Deer will stand and look at the automobile and not become frightened as long as the machine keeps going. Let it come to a stop and the deer are gone.

The same situation is true with the Pak-Jak and the other principal motorscooter, the Tote Gote. People who rode those during the hunting season told of riding right up on deer who watched the contraptions with mild curiosity and didn't start running until the hunter brought his machine to a stop.

This, despite the fact that the air-cooled motors make a considerable racket and the game must have heard the vehicle approaching for many minutes before it came in sight.

The situation, however, was different down in this canyon in Baja California. It soon became evident that game down here, unaccustomed even to the sight of human beings, knew nothing about gasoline motors, and as our five Pak-Jaks came roaring up the canyon, the sound of the motors echoing from the walls, the game simply took off.

As I walked up above our camp I became painfully aware of what had been happening. The story was all too plainly written in the sand.

In places this sand was quite damp where water was just beneath the surface. In one or two places there were pools.

Everywhere the story was the same. There had been all sorts of game in the canyon earlier in the afternoon. The game had suddenly taken off in fright and this had undoubtedly been due to the noise of the Pak-Jaks.

A typical view of the palm-lined canyon.

There were the tracks of mountain sheep, cat tracks, fox tracks, deer tracks, and, in the softer sand, tracks that I couldn't be sure of but which I thought were lion tracks. But there were lots of tracks. The canyon was alive with game.

It is interesting to note that Lee Sine and Ynes, who were on ahead of me, not only saw these tracks but after they had walked far enough to get away from the noise of camp and Pak-Jaks, found five mountain sheep standing watching them curiously.

They also found a ledge with faint Indian writings on it — writings that were all but faded out by wind and weather.

They reported that they were getting into a really interesting part of the canyon when it became so late that they knew they had to turn back, and even then they arrived in camp after dark.

I was bone weary that night as I crawled into my sleeping bag and I drifted off to sleep almost instantly.

Later on I wakened to watch the stars and marvel at the dryness of the air which brought so many stars into view that the whole heavens seemed to be one massive Milky Way.

I went to sleep again and wakened with a start. Some big animal was moving cautiously within a few feet of me.

I could hear the soft footfall of a cautious foot on gravel, then a rock moved under the weight of an animal that must have had some size.

I thought of the stories I had heard of mountain lions and lay motionless, listening.

The animal was also motionless for a moment, perhaps because it realized I was holding my breath. Then the animal moved on again through the darkness, perhaps thirty or forty feet from my bed, walking along the loose rock which had tumbled down from the mountain, making just enough rock noise so that I could be sure that it was an animal of some weight. But aside from those little noises of moving rocks and the previous noise of crunching gravel there had been no sound. Whatever the animal was, it was moving on padded feet and was keenly aware of the fact that I was lying awake, listening.

I lay there trying to determine whether the animal had gone and in the middle of my listening must have fallen sound asleep because when I awakened again the lopsided moon had turned the fronds of the palms into silver reflectors. The shadows were black in the canyon and here and there was a glimpse of moonlit sand.

There was complete silence — no sound of any sort — just the silence stretching from interstellar space down to the earth.

I enjoyed the sheer beauty of the spectacle, then closed my eyes again and was almost instantly enveloped in warm slumber.

5

The Mystery of the Burned Palms

We were up at the crack of dawn and after a hurried breakfast we left the others to get the camp packed up and loaded and we Pak-Jakkers went down the canyon to the intersection, then turned at the intersection and went up past the lone palm tree, then on up the other canyon.

Here we found varied scenery of breath-taking beauty. There were palms of all ages and all sizes. In places the canyon was nearly choked with palms.

And there were places that needed exploring badly; interesting branch canyons, outcroppings of rocks, veins — apparently of quartz — and a silent, majestic beauty.

As the canyon twisted and turned the light came from different angles and each clump of palms seemed to be more beautiful than the last. We knew that we should turn back in order to meet the mules and burros, but we kept on and on until finally we had to turn back.

We ride up a palm bordered wash which, within modern times, no human being has ever explored.

There are some facts that definitely limit one's choice of conduct. Hunger is one. We were out of provisions. Because we hadn't known if we could find good drinking water, we had gone light on groceries in order to carry water. Even so, the dangers of the trip being what they were, we were still just a little apprenhensive as we started back.

However, Lee Sine, J. W. Black and Emery opened their throttles wide and went tearing on up the canyon for another mile or so in a last-minute sprint.

The sheer beauty of those canyons held us entranced. Looking at the palms on the way back gave us a different view than we had had coming up, and the difference in lighting made each view seem completely novel. Only the telltale tracks of the mule train and our Pak-Jaks in the soft sand showed that anyone had ever been that way before.

It was some place along in here that Emery, who is intensely observing, made a discovery which was destined

Murl Emery finds a prospector's pick, the handle so checked by weather that it is apparent it had been out in the sun for many years. Later on we learned the almost incredible story associated with this pick.

to assume a great deal of significance later on, although at the time we simply considered it a puzzling find.

As has previously been pointed out, Murl Emery is quite an individualist. He does things his own way, at his own time, in his own manner, and while we were exploring the canyon Murl would make short side trips, would stop to look at rocks, would fall behind and usually catch up with us about the time we were stopping to take pictures.

Murl's find on this occasion was a geologist's pick, a characteristic tool which has a hammer on one end for knocking specimens off rocks and a sharp pick on the other for prying or digging.

This particular geologist's pick, or miner's pick, had been drawn to a point in some blacksmith's shop. This drawing out or sharpening of the end of the prospector's pick must have taken place very shortly before it had been lost by whoever had left it in the canyon, because apparently it had been used very little since the point had been drawn out.

At that time we hadn't heard the story of the two prospectors, the lost gold mine or the fatal rattlesnake bite. We didn't realize we had found the missing link — the prospector's pick.

From the way in which the handle had been checked and split by the dry air and the intense sunlight we knew this tool had been there for many years, mute evidence that some prospector had gone at least that far up the canyon.

It was only after we returned to Bahia de Los Angeles and saw the excitement Emery's find generated that we got the whole story and knew that pick had been lying there for twenty-nine years — lying in plain sight — and that four men had lost their lives trying to get up to where the pick had been lost.

At that time we only knew Emery had made a most

puzzling discovery. Any prospector who had managed to get that far up the canyon would have considered his prospector's pick as important as his canteen. It was unbelievable that such a person could simply have "lost" his pick.

Later on as we sat around the campfire, we tried to visualize what must have happened. We had all sorts of theories: The man had perhaps managed to get a burro into the canyon. He had tied the prospector's pick to the pack and it had fallen to the sand. Despite the fact we explored what we felt were all the possibilities our imaginations stopped far short of the real story. It proved to be a startling demonstration of the old saying that truth is stranger than fiction.

Somewhere near the point where Emery found that prospector's pick there is a fabulously rich gold mine.

And now we encountered another major mystery.

The men who had been with us knew these canyons. That is they knew the country surrounding the canyons.

The Pak-Jaks thunder along. Left to right: Murl Emery, Sam Hicks, J. W. Black and Lee Sine

They had known this country intimately for eighteen years. During that time they were positive no one had ever gone up into the parts of the canyon we were exploring. They couldn't have even made an attempt to reach the mountains which buttressed the canyons without using a known point for the initial supplies of water, food and animals for transportation.

Yet we found a goodly percentage of palm trees which had been burned.

As the palm trees grow, the leaves which constitute the frond wither and droop, forming a yellowish tinder-dry "skirt" around the trunk of the palm. Sometimes during periods of high wind these dead leaves are broken off and form a litter around the base of the palm trees. Under ordinary circumstances, however, the palms generally develop a "skirt" which stretches almost from the ground to the top of the palm; perhaps fifty or sixty feet of dry skirt; and the older part of this skirt at the bottom of the tree must be of great age.

A palm tree has a porous, resilient trunk. During the last war, bunkers made of palm logs proved to be more resistant to certain types of cannon fire than concrete.

There was plenty of mute evidence in our canyons that the trunks of the palm trees were so constituted that even when the skirts had been fired and had become a roaring inferno of swirling flames, the palm tree although badly damaged would eventually "come back" and again start growing.

So when we saw numerous palm trees which had virtually no skirts but fire-blackened trunks, we came to the conclusion that regardless of what the others had said someone *must* have been in those canyons within the last few years and fired the palm trees.

Juanito was very bitter about these burned palms. He

said that too many of the Mexican prospectors would glee-
fully set fire to palm trees in order to watch the spectacle,
having no concern for the beauty of the country — yet he
was also absolutely positive that no one had been up these
canyons for eighteen years.

On the other hand, Juanito's theory, if true, couldn't
account for all of the burned palms that we saw. As Emery
expressed it, "There aren't that many matches in the
country."

Studying the terrain through binoculars, we found isolated palm trees growing high on ledges in the boulder-
strewn mountains where it was unthinkable anyone would
have climbed simply for the purpose of setting fire to a
palm tree. In fact some of these palms grew in places where
it seemed almost impossible for any human being to travel.
Yet these isolated palms were the ones that were almost
uniformly burned.

Experimenting with some dead palm trees and with
some of the older leaves, which had dropped to the ground,
we found the material was all but explosive. Touch a
match to the bottom part of the skirt of a dead palm and
almost within the winking of an eye the whole tree would
be enveloped in flame.

Not only are the palm leaves like tinder but the skirts
are so arranged that there is a natural updraft. For a second
or so smoke will come swirling up through these palm
leaves, as though through some big chimney, then flickering
flames will dance through the white smoke and then the
whole tree becomes a roaring inferno and all this takes
place within a second or two.

Not only do the palm leaves burn, but the burning generates a highly-inflammable gas, which goes up high above
the tree and is then ignited, so that the column of flame
is many times higher than the tree itself.

119

Quite obviously, any material as explosive as this is a natural fire risk.

We subsequently learned that lightning accounts for many of these burned trees. In this granite country there are thunderstorms of great violence. Some are accompanied by rain, but as a rule the lighning comes first, the rain afterwards. And in many instances the electrical storm is a dry storm with little or no rain.

We collected evidence indicating that there is still another way in which the trees catch fire and this probably is due to static electricity, and the sparks generated by this static electricity.

There are winds in this country, dry winds, and so much static electricity that one must be careful, particularly if wearing rubber-soled shoes. Just the act of walking will build up quite a static charge and if one touches metal, or even another person, a hot spark will leap from the finger-tips.

Apparently during periods of high wind the rubbing of these palm fronds generates a charge of static electricity which at times can result in a spark, and one spark is all that is necessary to start this highly inflammable material going up in roaring flame.

Francisco Munoz told us that many times on his flights he has seen palm trees burning when careful inspection had convinced him there was no person anywhere around. He had studied these burning palms and the surrounding terrain sufficiently to convince himself that there is some form of spontaneous combustion which sets the trees afire.

The fact that some of the burning was due to lightning, was all too evident in trees where one would find only a portion of the skirts burned. These skirts are so highly inflammable that if the initial spark hadn't been followed almost immediately by a veritable deluge of water, as from a cloudburst, the entire skirt of the tree would have gone up in flames.

Apparently some of the palms can't "come back" after one of these devastating fires. We saw quite a few tall palms whose trunks had been denuded by fire and the tip of the tree was a barren, fire-blackened point. Some of these were standing, some had been blown over. Of course we had no way of knowing that those denuded trees which were still standing wouldn't eventually come back, since the palm is certainly tenacious and the porous moisture-absorbent trunk seems able to withstand almost any kind of abuse.

Juanito's familiarity with the canyons was as I mentioned earlier, due to the fact that he had worked on a ranch up in the mountains and had simultaneously carried on his shark fishing operations at the mouth of the wash. The total distance between the ranch and the camp at the mouth of the wash was something over twenty-five miles and Juanito walked it back and forth for two years at intervals, stopping at the oasis known as Agua Buena as his half-way point.

Trudging twenty-five miles up through loose sand, with the sun beating down from the walls of a canyon, then working on a ranch, turning around and walking twenty-five miles back to the ocean to engage in the arduous business of shark fishing, is indicative of Juanito's spirit.

I learned later on some of the things Juanito had done, some of the things he had been forced to do. The story made me squirm just to think of it, yet it is authenticated although it seems utterly incredible.

Juanito and one companion went up into a wide wash near Bahia San Luis Gonzaga and prospected up to the point where the wash became a canyon. They found indications of gold at the surface and Juanito and his companion started to sink shafts.

The soil was gravel and decomposed granite. They had no timbers with which to wall the shaft. They had to walk twelve miles to get their drinking water.

They rigged up a windlass and a bucket and tried to get down to bedrock. Juanito was the underground man. The other fellow turned the windlass. The holes were as small as they could be made, and Juanito, pushing down the hole, would have to stand with his feet on each side of the bucket as he filled it with gravel. Then the gravel would be put up, sifted, and the gold extracted by a dry cleaning process.

Juanito got down forty-two feet before he had to give up. He wasn't at bedrock at that time. He had reason to believe that bedrock might be another forty feet below him. At a depth of forty-two feet he felt that he was deep enough so he could risk lateral tunnels without too much danger of a cave-in, so he branched out with lateral tunnels. They put down other shafts and connected the lateral tunnels. These tunnels were very small. Juanto burrowed, as he expressed it, "like a rat."

They had no means of getting fresh air down the shafts. Moreover, much of the oxygen was consumed by an acetylene miner's lamp which Juanito was using.

Slowly, laboriously, facing the constant danger of a cave-in which would leave him buried alive, Juanito gophered around in the soil, scraping out a bucketful at a time which his companion, a strongly-built, powerful man, would raise on the windlass, put the dirt through a screen, process it in a dry washing process and extract the gold.

It can be imagined how these men lived. Their food consisted of tortillas and frijoles and very little else.

All in all they spent six weeks at this work and emerged with a pound of gold. As Juanito aptly remarked, "I have worked hard — too hard perhaps."

It is surprising what human beings can do when they have to in order to survive, when, as Emery expresses it, "the chips are down." Now, at the age of seventy-one, his short body bent by age and hard work, Juanito continues to work hard in order to make a living — too hard.

On this trip he would be up at the first streaks of daylight, building a little campfire, getting out his frying pans, cooking breakfast, then washing the dishes as best he could in the limited amount of water which we dared to allot for the purpose; then helping with the packing, climbing aboard a burro, riding all day, then, as we made camp just before dark, getting his fire going, his frying pans out and cooking a meal for nine hungry men over a campfire in the dark, hunkered down on his knees bending over the coals as he cooked.

Then later on he would gather up the dishes, take the frying pan half full of water which was all we dared spare for dishwashing and getting the dishes as clean as was possible under the circumstances, putting a few drops of water in the dish to rinse it out, then cleaning the dish and putting it out to dry.

After that, Juanito would get up from his knees, wearily walk over to the place where he had his blankets spread on the bare ground, crawl into "bed" and go to sleep.

Ynes, the younger of the two men, was really in the prime of life. He had the energy of a bouncing ball, and as I have said, the keenest pair of binocular eyes I have ever seen on anyone.

Ynes could not only see objects with his naked eye almost as plainly as I could see them with a pair of binoculars but he could, and did, see everything. Everything that moved Ynes saw, and I think he saw most of the things that didn't move; but the faintest flicker of motion anywhere and Ynes' eyes were on the spot, cataloguing what was going on.

123

The machines hoisted bit by bit, a step at a time, up the perpendicular, rocky wall.

Ynes not only made the long daily journeys and helped pack and unpack the burros, but he made innumerable side excursions. He walked, he rode burros, he doubled with Sam on the back of Sam's Pak-Jak.

I think what happened on the last day of our canyon trip is probably as indicative of the character of Ynes as anything I can use as an illustration.

We were traveling rapidly now, and we retraced our steps up to the sheer rock wall. We were carrying ropes with us and were quite a distance ahead of the mules and burros.

Those Pak-Jaks weigh a hundred and seventy-five pounds apiece in the raw. In addition to that we had saddlebags which were pretty well loaded but which could of course be removed as we came to this vertical portage.

124

Ynes worked his way up the rock face with all the facility of a mountain goat. Sam Hicks joined him. Lee Sine followed.

J. W. Black worked the Pak-Jaks, one by one, up to the bottom of the rocky wall. Then Black picked up the front end of each Pak-Jak and knotted around it the rope which the others had lowered from above. Then Black picked up the lower part of the Pak-Jak, braced himself, heaved his powerful muscles and lifted the Pak-Jak up to a point where it was in the proper position for the others to start hauling on the rope.

There were five Pak-Jaks in all. They had to be raised up the perpendicular face of the rock. Then our gear, stowed in the saddlebags, had to be lifted up.

By that time the train of mules and burros had arrived and all of the camp gear was unloaded and it had to be hoisted up by ropes. Then the unladen burros were taken back down the canyon to a point where they could scramble up the rocky slope and be guided up over the high ridge until they were able to get down into the canyon above the rocky barrier. Here they were repacked.

Ynes assisted in all of this, working at top speed.

Sam Hicks, J. W. Black and Lee Sine, all rugged outdoor men, kept pace with Ynes and the Mexicans and in so doing earned their respect.

By the time we had our equipment assembled at the top of the rocky wall it was well along in the afternoon.

Sam Hicks and Lee Sine started ahead on their Pak-Jaks. Ynes, using his coat as a cushion, climbed on behind Sam and they started off up the wash at top speed.

By that time it was apparent we weren't going to be able to get too far before we had to make a camp, and we were completely out of provisions. We had no coffee, no frijoles. In fact we had nothing.

I tried to keep up with Sam and Lee, but they were going too fast. Not only was the gear ratio of their machines such that they were a shade faster than mine, but these men with their perfect sense of balance, rhythm and coordination could take many of the rough places at full throttle, whereas I had to slow down. So I came along behind moving as rapidly as I dared, but taking no chances since a broken bone in that country would have presented us with an almost insurmountable problem.

Some distance behind me J. W. Black was keeping pace with Murl Emery and behind them came the mules and burros.

Sam and Lee hoped they would be able to get to the mountain barrier early enough so they could "ride" their Pak-Jaks over the trail, down to camp, get emergency rations from the stock we had left in the tent, and hike back over the trail to a point where they could join the camp.

As it happened, I wasn't fully familiar with the plans. All I knew was that Sam, Lee and Ynes had gone on ahead, that the rest of the camp was somewhere behind me. So I just kept plodding along.

Quite late in the afternoon I reached a point in the sandy wash where I could go no further. I was in a cactus country where balls of cactus spines on the ground would puncture a front tire if we ran over them — as we had earlier found out to our sorrow. I was also in a country where the rocks which had rolled down from the mountain barrier were getting bigger and bigger and at times it was necessary to lift the rear end of the machine when it would get straddled over some big rock.

Lifting the heavy rear end of a machine which weighs nearly two hundred pounds, time after time, is simply too much of a good thing for a man who is not accustomed to heavy lifting of that sort, who has had a full day of Pak-Jak travel and the excitement of exploration.

I decided that I could make better time walking than I could on the Pak-Jak so I simply abandoned the Pak-Jak, knowing that somehow or another I had missed the trail — not knowing exactly where the trail was, and with my lifting muscles pretty well worn out.

So I walked up the mountain barrier. I never did find that darned trail. I simply climbed the side of the mountain, a few feet at a time, until I came to the mesa on top. Then I knew that the trail was plainly legible so I moved along until I saw the characteristic sign of the trail, one or two rocks piled on top of a really big rock, making a sort of rude monument.

I worked my way over, found the trail and wearily continued along the mesa, then started down the "trail" on the other side.

Halfway down the trail I met Sam and Lee coming back up. I was surprised to see them. I thought they had planned to spend the night at the tent.

They had a pretty good-sized sack of provisions, which Sam was carrying over his shoulder.

It was then only fifteen or twenty minutes before sunset and night comes quickly in that country. There was, moreover, no moon until around one or two o'clock in the morning.

So it was quickly decided that Lee Sine would go back to the tent with me and we hoped we could find enough covering there to keep us warm during the night. If we couldn't, there was a stove in the tent and we could rustle firewood and so keep warm as long as we stayed up to stoke the stove.

So Sam, with the heavy sack over his shoulder, his long legs devouring the ground, walked rapidly on up the trail.

The ground was well-covered with broken cacti—their spines, stiff as nails and sharp as needles, would penetrate a shoe or puncture a tire.

I asked where Ynes was and Sam told me that he had decided to stay "on top" for a little while.

Ynes had of course simply stepped off the Pak-Jak at the foot of the mountain trail, had walked up to the top, and was up there in the top country some place, his keen eyes surveying everything that had happened. He had of course seen me come up on the Pak-Jak, wrestle it for half a mile or so over a series of rocks where I had to keep lifting and straining, and at the same time keep in mind the necessity of avoiding the balls of spines on the ground.

These particular balls of cactus had stiff, unbelievably sharp spines which were some three inches long, would go through shoe leather as if it were paper, and had given us a couple of punctures on the front tires.

I explained to Sam where I had left my Pak-Jak and told Sam that when he got over the mountain he could pick up my Pak-Jak and ride it down to meet the others. In that way he might get there before it got too dark to see any obstacles which might be in his path.

When Sam got over the top of the mountain barrier and started down the trail on the other side he met Ynes pushing my Pak-Jak. It is difficult to explain what this means so that a person who is not familiar with the Pak-Jak can realize what Ynes was doing.

There is no free wheeling on a Pak-Jak. The whole secret of the thing is an arrangement of gears and sprockets by which a three and a half horsepower air-cooled motor furnishes the power that can hold the front wheel of a Pak-Jak up against a solid wall while the hind wheel will continue to revolve slowly and steadily until it digs a hole.

When one starts pushing a machine of that kind it is necessary to push against the motor, and while at times the belt can be loosened enough to avoid the full compression of the motor, there is always a drag.

Moreover, when one is standing on one side holding the handle bars and trying to push this machine, it is necessary to exert a great deal of strength in order to keep the machine from toppling over on the other side.

Bear in mind that this machine, weighing a hundred and seventy-odd pounds, has to be kept on balance. If it gets too far off on one side it is simply going to topple over and carry a man with it.

Now Ynes had been *pushing* my machine for over half a mile across a cactus-infested country, and lifting it over great lava rocks, in order to reach the trail at the foot of the mountain barrier. Then he had started pushing it *up* the trail.

Riding a Pak-Jak is difficult enough over these rocks

where one has enough traction to keep the rear wheel turning. In such cases the machine has only to be lifted over rocks which are big enough to leave the frame suspended with the wheel off the ground and in such a position they have no traction. But to *push* a machine over these rocks is something very few men could do and even then a hundred yards would leave them completely exhausted.

Ynes had been pushing my machine for more than half a mile to get to the foot of the mountain barrier and now he was *pushing* it up the trail — and all this after a day of arduous labor, a day which would have left most men physically exhausted.

So now Sam climbed on my machine, Ynes folded his coat and got on behind Sam, and with the sack of provisions the men started back over the half-mile or so of rough, rocky terrain strewn with boulders and cactus spines, and then down the soft, sandy wash for some two or three miles until they could see the glow of the campfire which guided them into the camp where hungry men eagerly pounced on the provisions Sam and Lee had hurriedly thrown in the sack.

I subsequently found out that on several occasions Ynes had been up "on top" so he could watch me as I explored around the country. He kept me under almost constant supervision.

As he was heard to express it to one of his companions, he never "bothered" me because he saw that I was "all right."

I know now that if at any time I had sprained an ankle, broken a leg, or had any other mishap, Ynes would have been at my side within a matter of minutes. And if I had a broken ankle I know very well that Ynes would have piggybacked me over the roughest mountain terrain and got me back to camp.

It is loyalty of this sort that leaves a man feeling a little choked up. It is a loyalty that was far above and beyond the call of duty connected with employment. These men had given us their friendship and it was remarkable to see the extent of their loyal devotion.

6

Enter the Helicopter

Lee Sine and I went on down the trail to the tent.

It was a rather dispiriting sight as we arrived in the late dusk and picked up one of the electric lanterns.

The wind had been blowing through this mountain pass almost constantly. One side of the tent had broken loose from the anchoring stakes and had been flapping back and forth, whipping the desiccated soil into a flour-fine dust which had covered everything in the tent with a layer that seemed to be a quarter of an inch thick.

We built a fire in the stove. We dusted off some of the boxes. We cleared off a space on the table. We found that there was no gasoline in the gasoline lantern and we were just too plain, damned tired to try and get a gasoline can open, find a funnel and get the gasoline lantern filled.

We used electric flashlights to cook up a small dinner. We scouted around and found what covering there was in camp—a part of a sleeping bag which had been left by Emery, a quilt which had been left by Juanito, and some canvas.

We made up a couple of beds and, keeping all of our clothes on, rolled in to sleep before six-thirty.

We awakened during the night and found that we were thoroughly chilled. We built a fire in the stove and got the tent good and warm, drifted off to sleep again, then woke up sometime around midnight and repeated the process.

This time we had the stove pretty well filled with coals and the chill was broken until around four o'clock in the morning when we again built up the fire.

By daylight we cooked up a breakfast and then went out to thaw out in the sun while we waited for the others to show up.

Soon we heard the familiar roar of Pak-Jaks and Sam, J. W. Black and Murl Emery came into camp. Shortly after the mules and burros arrived, we started hurriedly breaking camp, throwing things into the pickups, getting the tent down and rolled up, and then started the long, dusty grind back across the sandy washes, through the narrow canyons, down to the dry lakes, across the dry lakes and toward the road.

We arrived late in the afternoon at Bahia de Los Angeles. We were dirty, dusty and tired. I had a two weeks' growth of gray whiskers, I was gray with dust, I hadn't had a bath for more than a week. I was just plain, downright dirty.

The others were in the same condition.

We found a palatial yacht at anchor in the bay. We found a group of famous people on board and they were expecting our arrival because they had been told by Antero Diaz that we were about due. (Diaz had the news from the observations of "Faithful Francisco," who had kept us under fairly constant observation from the air.)

The party included a multi-millionaire and some famous literary people. One of them was Joe Krutch. As well-known for his nature writing as he is for his literary criticism and philosophical essays, he has a wonderful talent for describing country— a real eye for detail. His book on Baja California, for which he was collecting material at the time, has now been published.*

There was also Roger Tory Peterson, the famous artist and author of A Field Guide to the Birds. Peterson had just completed a new edition of A Field Guide to Western Birds and was now engaged in gathering material for still another book.

There were other people aboard the yacht, people who were friends of friends of mine, people who knew Murl Emery well, people who were friends of friends of J. W. Black and Lee Sine.

It would have been hard to have imagined circumstances under which we were less presentable, and after shaking hands and acknowledging introductions we got away as rapidly as possible to the luxury of a cold shower bath.

As I have previously mentioned, the shower baths at Bahia de Los Angeles are at times rather sketchy affairs. Not only is the "heating" of the water a problem, but there is no reserve supply of water. When several persons take showers at the same time the water dwindles to a trickle and then without further warning the trickle vanishes.

So, during times of peak activity at the showers, if a person doesn't move swiftly he is very apt to find he has covered his chilled skin with a thick lather of soap only to have insufficient water to wash it away.

By the time I could get into the showers the water was quite cold and the strain of all of us making simultaneous ablutions reduced the flow of water to a trickle, a dribble,

*The Forgotten Peninsula. Joseph Wood Krutch, — (Sloane, 1961.)

The gang takes time out to go fishing.

and then just a few scattered drops which could be collected in the cupped hands of the bather and applied where it would do the most good.

Nevertheless, I remember that cold shower as one of the nicest, most luxurious I had ever had.

And then came dinner at the Casa Diaz.

The showers at Bahia de Los Angeles may be rather primitive but as I've said before, the food is just about the best in the world. This evening, it was not only there in abundance, but it seemed especially succulent after our recent camp fare.

And after having existed on lukewarm water which had been sloshed around in canteens until it had acquired a metallic taste, the luxury of the carbonated Orange Crush which had been given us by Colonel Gutierrez as we left Mexicali, was beyond description. Our dehydrated tissues soaked up the tangy beverage and stomachs which had known only frijoles and tortillas for many days welcomed the flavor of citrus fruits. To people who had been rationed on lukewarm drinking water from canteens, this carbonated drink with its orange flavor was luxury beyond compare. We still had nearly a case of it left in the pickups and we "shot the works." The dinner at Casa Diaz was out of this world, and what with one thing and another we didn't get to bed until nearly eight-thirty that night. That was dissipation!

In the morning the people from the yacht came over to visit with us at breakfast. They had a twin-motored plane and were taking off for a quick flight down the peninsula, covering distances that would have taken us six or seven days by four-wheel drive automobile. They expected to be back at Bahia de Los Angeles by noon and then up-anchor and down the gulf on the yacht.

We saw them off in the plane, then loaded our gear and took off from Bahia de Los Angeles headed north.

It was with a real pang that we said good-by to our friends, at the Bahia de Los Angeles, people whom we had come to know and to respect, people who had shared risks with us and who had been devoted to our welfare.

I looked back as we left. Antero was waving good-by. Ynes, who is largely Yaqui Indian, was trying to be as expressionless as possible. Juanito was trying to smile a farewell but the tears were trickling down his weatherbeaten cheeks.

At the time, I had no idea we would ever be back.

In a limited way, we had achieved some of our objectives. We had gone into those canyons and we had made some hasty exploration. On the other hand, there was so much we hadn't achieved and it looked as though we never could. Transporting gasoline, drinking water, food and personnel by mule pack into a base camp in the canyon called for more equipment than was available.

We might establish a base camp on the dry lakes and have Pepe Smith go back and forth carrying supplies with mule and burro, but the mules and burros couldn't stand the strain. Those hardy little animals can go for two or perhaps three days without water while they are being worked, but they can't keep up a pace of that sort, living off the country and being rationed on water. Moreover, even with our four-wheel drive trucks we couldn't carry enough water to the dry lakes to keep the livestock supplied with their needs.

However, while we hadn't covered more than a small percentage of the canyon system, we had gone a good many miles up and down the canyons. We hadn't been able to do more than hit the high spots and hadn't had time for detailed exploration, but we had had adventures and we had experienced the satisfaction of knowing that we had managed to reach places other men had never explored.

So it happened as we pulled out of Bahia de Los Angeles

that I didn't expect to see Juanito, Ynes or Antero Diaz for many, many months, if ever. We had made our assault on the canyons and had probably reached a point where we could call it a draw. We hadn't conquered the canyons, but on the other hand the canyons hadn't conquered us. We had been in them. We had actually gone for some miles up the dreaded Sal Si Puede (Get out if you can), and we had got out.

But those canyons were in my blood. I kept thinking of them. I kept dreaming about them.

We got home and I developed my pictures. I found I had some striking photographs. I studied those photographs and from them made a rough map of the canyons. I plotted out about where we had been with our Pak-Jaks by checking the photographs taken from the air.

The daughter of Louis Roripaugh, who is one of my closest friends, was married to a helicopter pilot, who spent his time during the summer months piloting a helicopter for one of the big companies that is engaged in mining activities in Alaska and in Canada.

This young man came to visit us and brought pictures that he had taken from the helicopter. It was only natural that he should start talking about what a helicopter could do.

Instantly I became fired with enthusiasm. What were the chances of getting a helicopter to explore Baja California, to ferry supplies back and forth to a base camp in the Sal Si Puede Canyon?

The young pilot, Ron Frame, thought our chances were pretty good, *if* I wanted to spend the money. Helicopters, as it turned out, were pretty darned expensive.

At first I decided, therefore, that the idea of exploration by helicopter could be nothing more than an air castle. But that night as I tried to sleep I realized that expenses are, after all, only relative.

Cardone, circio and author's Land Rover.

Emery's car in colorful canyon.

A person would think nothing of spending three thousand dollars for a trip to Europe where he would be following the beaten trail of tourist routine. Or if some business situation arose where I had to go to New York, I would unhesitatingly bundle a couple of secretaries, typewriters and dictating machines into an airplane and take off on a trip which would cost much more than three thousand dollars, and three thousand dollars was the standard rental rate for the helicopter for two weeks.

After all, I was only young once so what the heck.

I arose in the morning after a more or less sleepless night, during which I had been haunted by dreams of canyon exploration, and grimly determined to see the thing through.

So I rang up Ron Frame and asked him if his company would consider a charter trip to Baja California.

Frame said he would find out and started putting through telephone calls.

A couple of days later Frame advised me that his company had turned it down. Their equipment was all too far north. They didn't want to transfer it to the south; but he gave me the names of other companies that were engaged in helicopter rentals.

I got busy on the telephone and found companies that were quite willing to charter helicopters—until they found out the terrain I had in mind, then instantly the warmth of cordial salesmanship was replaced by the cold chill of indifference.

In place of having them try to sell me I found that I was trying to sell them, and as buyers they were unbelievably cold — cordial personally but officially very, very cold.

A helicopter needs careful attention. It needs supplies and watchful maintenance. And a helicopter needs insurance. That is, a company chartering helicopters must have insurance.

Since Baja California is a country of very poor roads where little is known about existing conditions other than the fact that it is currently supposed to be a country of barren mountains, of arid deserts, of great winds and considerable turbulence, no one wanted to be the first to pioneer a helicopter exploration, and apparently the insurance companies regarded Baja California with jaundiced eyes.

Then Ron Frame paid a visit to the Hiller Aircraft Corporation which manufactures the Hiller helicopter.

This company considers their product to be a long step ahead of any competitive helicopter. They feel they have more power, more lift, more dependability; in short, just about more of everything, and they were interested in the idea of using the helicopter to lift our Pak-Jaks from a base camp on the dry lake to a spike camp in the canyons. They were also interested in hovering over country which had never before been explored. In short they were interested.

After some telephone conversations Bob Boughton, the young man who has charge of foreign sales, decided to come down and have a talk with me.

The result was to have been anticipated.

By this time my colored slides had been processed and I had the story of the canyons in color: Pictures taken at a great height from airplanes; pictures a little lower in airplanes; pictures showing the manner in which we had made our limited assault on the canyons; and a few precious pictures of the interior of the canyons, the beautiful palm trees, the intriguing rock walls, some of the veins of quartz.

Slowly, steadily, remorselessly, the story of those canyons as portrayed in my colored pictures, started working on Bob Boughton. By the time he was ready to start back to San Francisco, the canyon fever had fired his blood. He was all for it.

A couple of days later Bob was on the telephone. The

company had decided to work out a deal of joint exploration. It wasn't in the business of chartering helicopters, but it was in the business of demonstrating what its helicopters could do. The challenge of Baja California, the very things that had kept other companies from being interested, the wind, the turbulence, the difficulties, all were a challenge the Hiller Company wanted to meet. It was felt that we could work out the financial details and other problems so we could go in for a joint exploration.

So once more I threw my writing schedule out the window. I got busy on the telephone. J. W. Black closed up his Pak-Jak shop in Paradise. Murl Emery, who was engaged in an important mining deal, threw the whole thing overboard announcing that he never had cared for money anyway. Leo Roripaugh (a brother of Louis Roripaugh and an enthusiast on Baja California) offered to come along with a four-wheel drive pickup capable of carrying seven fifty-gallon drums of aviation gasoline.

Almost before I knew it and certainly before I had had an oportunity thoroughly to air my sleeping bag and unpack the dust-impregnated duffel bags I had brought back from my other trip, I was getting things together for just about the most exciting expedition I could imagine.

This one was going to be *it*. We were going to meet those canyons head on and beat them on their home ground.

It was decided that we would send ahead three four-wheel drive pickups, one Land Rover station wagon, all loaded with gasoline and supplies so as to enable us to cover the first leg of the trip as expeditiously as possible. Bob Boughton, Pedro Rivas, the helicopter maintenance man, and I would leave some hours later, pass the pickups on the road and fly on to the Hattie Hamilton place where we would rendezvous the first night.

Since I have an hour-long weekly television show it is

Bob Boughton.

almost necessary that no matter where I travel I keep one foot in Hollywood. So I had arranged with Francisco Munoz to come along with his airplane, to shuttle back and forth from the closest landing field to our various camps, to fly in scripts, important mail, extra supplies and secretarial replacements as needed.

All of my portable office equipment, portable typewriters, dictating machines, tape recorders, etc., were sent on ahead with the pickups.

Everything was set for departure early Monday morning and Bob Boughton promised to have the helicopter at the ranch sometime Sunday.

That Sunday was a day of hectic activity. Not only had I started dictating at three o'clock in the morning, trying to get my more pressing work caught up, but I had been up at four o'clock the morning before and had been pouring words into a dictating machine most of Saturday, taking only enough time out to do some rather hurried and sketchy packing.

On that Sunday, whenever I would hear the sound of an engine I would convince myself that this was the helicopter coming in for a landing, and would drop everything to run out and take a look.

As it happened, that Sunday there were numerous planes flying over the ranch, and I must have gone hurrying out at least fifteen different times, each time firmly expecting to see the helicopter hovering overhead.

By four o'clock in the afternoon I was certain it would be only a matter of minutes, and then after an hour or so of waiting, as the sun finally set, I found my disappointment giving way to very definite annoyance. I felt that Bob Boughton could at least have telephoned if he had encountered any unforeseen difficulties.

I quit work at five o'clock, left my study and walked up

Pete Rivas.

the hill to the main house. Murl Emery, Sam Hicks and J. W. Black were sitting in the front room having drinks. I joined them. Dusk was deepening into darkness. We gave way to the blues. Then suddenly we heard the sound of an engine, approaching rapidly and at a low elevation.

We rushed to the door, looked out, saw nothing, and then the helicopter burst into view coming in at not over a hundred feet above the ground. As we stood there, the landing lights came on.

There were high voltage wires running across the yard

by the house. It had never occurred to me that anyone would try to land a helicopter there in the yard, but now with darkness blanketing the country it was quite apparent from the way the helicopter hovered briefly that it was contemplating a landing.

I made a dash for a flashlight that had a red warning light on it, but before I had made more than half a dozen steps the helicopter settled down, not in the yard where we had expected it, but in front of the house and almost on the doorstep—a place, as it turned out, that Bob Boughton had scouted out on his earlier trip as being a safe landing spot.

It was an unusual experience. Five minutes earlier we had been moodily contemplating the wreckage of our scheduled trip. Now we were escorting Bob Boughton and Pedro (Pete) Rivas the few short steps from the helicopter into the living room.

I think it was perhaps at that time that I first began to realize the extent to which these canyons had been dominating my life. I wanted to get in those canyons and explore them from one end to the other, and when it looked as though our helicopter trip was going to be delayed or perhaps canceled, I had felt such a keen sense of personal failure that it seemed someone had pulled a plug and plunged my mind into darkness.

Now that the helicopter had arrived, the revulsion of feeling showed me how much the exploration of those canyons meant to me.

Long before daylight the next morning there was a great deal of activity at the ranch. Leo Roripaugh came over with his pickup and the machines pulled out for San Diego and Tijuana.

Bob Boughton, Pete Rivas and I, who were to go in the helicopter, were able to wait for what was planned as a leisurely breakfast. I gave a lot of last-minute instructions, got in the helicopter, strapped myself in and heard the roar of the engine as the machine started. I braced myself and waited.

Suddenly we shot up into the air.

Contrary to my expectations, there was no feeling of rising, none of the "cold stomach" of an elevator ascent. I felt that the ground had simply dropped away beneath us, and we poised for a moment, hovering over the ranch, then took off across the roofs of the ranch buildings just above the power lines, headed for the steep mountains back of the ranch.

There was one persistent and peculiar sensation connected with riding in that helicopter. I felt as if I were floating inside a huge soap bubble, and I'll admit there was a great feeling of insecurity. I kept waiting for the bubble to burst.

Looking down between my feet through the plexiglass I could see the ground not over forty or fifty feet below me. Above and to both sides there was only plexiglass.

Below me the mountainside was a streak of half-blurred panorama: The fire trails I had cut so arduously, the steep, precipitous, rocky slopes, the clumps of trees, the old spring, and then more rocks, all flowing past in a vast moving spectacle of unreality. I had climbed so laboriously up this very steep mountainside that I couldn't adjust myself to skimming up it at such speed so effortlessly.

Abruptly the ridge of the mountains was directly ahead. It looked as though we could just about clear it. Clear it, we did—and suddenly the whole country dropped away beneath me. I found myself suspended in space in a fragile soap bubble with a straight drop of a thousand feet directly beneath my seat.

It was for the moment a terrifying sensation.

We crossed the wide valley, hovered over the automobile highway, then left it as we took a compass course for Tijuana. Mountains loomed ahead. We made no attempt to get over the top of the mountains, but instead roared into the canyon.

I felt that I knew enough about flying to know that no mechanical contraption designed to take men through the air had any business going up this steep mountain valley; and particularly when Bob swung the machine over to within a few feet of the canyon walls, I felt my time had come.

I learned afterwards that this is good helicopter technique. Entering a canyon where there is a wind blowing, one hugs the steep slope up which the wind is being pushed by the pressure of currents and simply rides the updraft to the top of the mountain, thereby saving fuel and power.

I finally realized that we were being buoyed up as we came so close to this steep slope and the air cushion sent us zooming upward, and then just as I had relaxed and had accustomed myself to that feeling of being lifted by the wind, we were over the top and again the country fell out from beneath me. Again I was poised over a sheer drop.

It was hard to keep from tensing one's muscles under those circumstances. I darn near pushed the floor out.

By the time we had reached the outskirts of San Diego, however, I had adjusted myself pretty much to the sensation and was beginning to look around and enjoy myself.

Skimming along so close to the ground gives one the true feeling of flying and discloses things that would never be visible to a person traveling in a conventional airplane.

For instance, as we came up the slope of one of the hills we encountered a big hawk sitting in the branches of an oak tree. Apparently he had a belligerent personality, or else he was familiar with helicopters, because he didn't make any attempt to fly. He simply sat there and fixed us with a cold,

148

SANTA INÉS

TO ENSENADA

NA CHAPALA

PUNTA FINAL

GOLFO DE CALIFORNIA

N

AGUA BUENA
SPRING CAMPSITE

CERRO DOS
PICACHOS

LA ASAMBLEA

AGUA SODA

CAMPSITE

SAL SI PUEDE

MAIN ROAD

Isla Angel de la Guarda

Punta Remedios

CAMPSITE
AND AIRSTRIP

Dry Lake

RUINS OF
DESENGAÑO

Dry Lake

PUNTA PRIETA

Bahía de Los Angeles

TO LA PAZ

PACIFIC OCEAN

Here where there are no Roads
or Trails... NO ONE should
try to explore here except with
Pak Jak, Tote Gote or ample
Air Support.

MacD

baleful eye, apparently speculating on whether we were too big to eat.

For a moment his head and eye were in my field of vision, then he was gone and we were gliding on up the slope, riding the cushion of air thrust up by the wind.

Almost before I realized it we had flown over the outskirts of San Diego, had left the city behind and were crossing the border. A short time later we came down at the Tijuana airport.

Here we had our first point of assembly. Francisco Munoz was waiting with his plane to take Jean, my chief secretary, to the Hattie Hamilton Ranch, a hundred and twenty miles below Ensenada, and nearly two hundred miles south of the border.

We had found that we couldn't take drums of aviation gasoline across the border without a special permit, so we had decided to buy aviation gasoline at Tijuana and load the pickups at that point. There were crossing formalities to delay us briefly and all in all it was well past mid-morning when we again entered the helicopter and started the motor.

Once more I had that feeling of the ground falling away beneath me and then we were headed south, slightly to the east of the main business district of Tijuana.

From that helicopter I began to realize for the first time the extent to which Tijuana had grown. It was not only bursting at the seams, but had spread all over the surrounding country with residential districts creeping up the sides of the hills, fanning out in every direction.

Then we had passed Tijuana and were gliding along over the ocean.

Between Tijuana and Ensenada there are some beautiful secluded beaches, and we found many house trailers parked along them, and occasionally saw vacationing families in tents.

Once as we came to a high bluff and dropped down to within a few feet of the ocean, we came on a party of bathing beauties basking in the sunlight. They looked up in startled surprise, then collected their senses in time to wave cordially as we went sliding by.

That of course brought a question to my mind. I leaned over to Bob and said, "Bob, what will we do if we come on girls sunbathing in the nude?"

Bob's answer was laconic and typical of a helicopter pilot.

"Stop," he said.

For a moment I had to adjust myself to the idea that with this helicopter we could instantly pause in our flight, hover over any object we wanted to look at, and then if it suited our convenience drop gently to the ground as a bird would put down his legs and light on the branch of a tree.

This was the true sensation of flying.

I have spent lots of time in airplanes over the years. In fact my first passenger flight had been in 1916 or 1917, when going up in an airplane was really a hazardous adventure. Yet here in this helicopter I was for the first time truly experiencing flying.

We skirted Ensenada and again I had an opportunity to observe the tremendous growth which had taken place in the past few years, particularly the development of the harbor. Then we were headed south toward the Hattie Hamilton Ranch, and again for a while were out over the ocean.

A seal that had been sunning himself on a rock hastily slipped into the water. We rounded a point and came on a flock of cormorants that broke into sudden panic-stricken flight.

Some of them tried to dodge. One of them tried to outfly the helicopter, and when he found out that he couldn't did the next best thing: he plunged headlong into the water in full flight and at high speed, and submarined himself.

I have, etched in my mind, a picture of that frightened bird, looking back over his shoulder, so to speak, and then making a dive for the water, going in "wide open." I saw him push out one webbed foot in order to break the force of the impact. I suppose the other one was also out, but his body concealed it.

That cormorant must have felt very much like a water skiier who is suddenly plunged into the water at high speed—and skiiers who have had that experience tell me the surface of the water feels like concrete when they hit.

It had been years since I had been at the Hamilton Ranch and I found out that I am completely lost in the air. Landmarks which are thoroughly familiar on the ground flatten out once I get up in the air, and the whole countryside somehow looks different. Some people have a high degree of air orientation. I haven't.

Munoz with his airplane was cruising at almost twice our speed, since ours was cut down due to the excess load we were carrying: baggage racks on the side, extra gasoline tanks, an emergency supply kit of food and several gallons of water.

We were going into a country where one just doesn't take any unnecessary chances, and while all of this equipment slowed us down, it gave us added comfort and an additional margin of safety.

Munoz, however, had to stop in Ensenada to get some official papers and so it happened that we both reached the Hamilton Ranch at about the same time.

Margo Cesena, who operates the Hattie Hamilton Ranch, is a remarkable character. Tall, vital, competent, freedom-loving and independent, she operates the ranch just as much by herself as is physically possible.

152

She manages the ranch, supervises the comfort of the guests, does the cooking and the serving, cleans up and washes the dishes, and all the time carries on a running fire of conversation, keeping everyone cheerful, moving with the skilled efficiency of an artist who has learned to make every move count.

Margo is a colorful character and it is well worth a trip to the Hamilton Ranch simply to visit with her and hear her cheerful laugh, her voice raised in song as she goes about her work, and to listen to her comments on the activities of the countryside, her latest trip to Ensenada, and her thoughts about life generally.

There was to be a birthday party fiesta in the neighborhood and not only was Margo going, but the hosts had been kind enough to invite our party to be present.

So we all piled into a truck and Margo drove us through the darkness, jolting around over the dirt roads, until finally I lost all sense of direction.

After some thirty minutes we pulled up in front of a lighted house which was literally bursting with people, and went inside.

There was the inevitable stringed orchestra supplemented by a cornet. There was laughter and motion and dancing, and there were some very beautiful women and some very courteous men.

A man who could have been cast for a typical Spanish Don hunted me up to shake my hand. "This is my house," he said. "I own it. It is yours," and then he gripped my hand again and took me into the dining room where quite a feast had been laid out buffet style.

"My turkey," he said, indicating the huge browned bird on the table, "will fly no more."

And he beamed with pride at the thought of being able to provide such hospitality for his guests.

This was an intimate party. The friends around the countryside had gathered to make a festive occasion and to do honor to the host and hostess. We were rank outsiders. These people knew each other, understood each other, understood each other's customs, and had many things in common.

We were persons of another race. Our language was somewhat strange to them and with the deference of persons who were self-conscious about making a mistake, they hesitated to talk except to make simple statements.

There were, moreover, many of the *vaqueros* there who knew no English at all. They had never seen us before, we were strangers and if we wanted to be blunt about it, intruders on their festivities. We had been asked because we were the guests of Margo.

But we were treated as honored guests. They went out of their way to show us their feelings of friendship. It was a warm, congenial gathering and while under the circumstances I felt that common courtesy required that we return to the ranch and to bed at an early hour, there was the feeling that the country had opened its doors and its hearts to us.

Our party of helicopter adventurers stayed only a couple of hours or so and then Margo accompanied us back to the Hamilton Ranch. Margo returned and stayed until the party broke up which was, I believe, sometime around three-thirty in the morning. She was, I understand, an active participant. Yet when I was up at six o'clock I heard the sound of the coffee pot being put on the stove and a moment later, Margo's voice raised in song as she started cooking breakfast.

#7

A True Flying Experience

We had several objectives for our trip south.

We wanted to visit those palm-lined canyons we had seen in the northern district as well as to explore La Asemblea and Sal Si Puede in greater detail. We also wanted to land where we could take a look at a wrecked airplane we had seen on our trip of exploration with Francisco Munoz.

This plane had made a forced landing and had been abandoned far up in the high mesa country near the backbone of the peninsula. It had contained two people who had been able to "walk away" from the scene of the landing.

What happened after that was tragic.

Since they were on the backbone of the peninsula, they had the choice of going in either of two directions, but the route to the east seemed the shorter; they could see the gulf from where they had landed and it was probably not more than twenty miles in an air line to the gulf, although the intervening country was exceedingly rough.

155

Looking down on a wrecked plane.

Hovering over a palm-lined canyon.

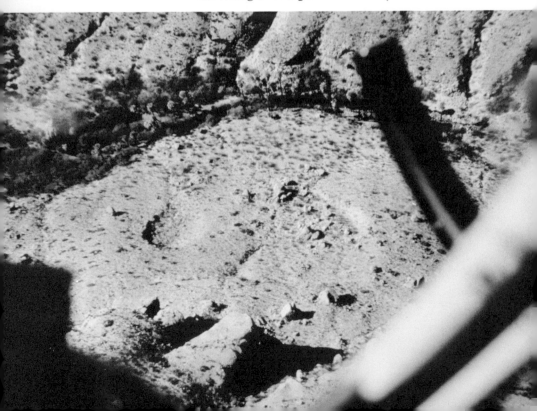

To the west however it was perhaps forty miles to the ocean in an air line.

So probably after some considerable discussion, the two men had started east, trying to intersect the road which stretched south from Puertecitos.

They never made it.

Not only had they died of thirst, but when eventually their bodies were found they had become so completely dehydrated that the bodies had mummified and were found in that condition only a relatively short distance from the road they had been trying to reach.

The irony of the situation was that our exploration from the helicopter indicated that if they had headed to the west they needed only to have gone a mile and a half to have encountered a canyon with shade and good drinking water, and from there on they could have worked their way down to the road, having water all the way until they were within perhaps ten or twelve miles of reasonably level going.

Viewed from a high elevation it seemed that the light plane might well be intact, and because there was a terrific downdraft over this part of the peninsula the abandoned plane was always viewed from several thousand feet.

We decided to make an inspection of this plane one of the first of our objectives.

However, our planned schedule was interrupted by bad news. It seemed that when our trucks reached Ensenada the drivers learned Ensenada was having a "fiesta." The government offices were all closed and would probably be closed for another two or three days. As a result, the drivers of the pickups couldn't get the necessary clearance, tourist card permits, etc. So instead of meeting us at Hattie Hamilton's as had been planned, the members of our party and all the reserve supplies were being held up in Ensenada and might be held there for another two or three days.

Exploring a palm-lined canyon.

The trip had been so carefully planned and the time element was so important that this was in the nature of a major calamity, but Francisco Munoz who "knew the ropes" felt certain that he could fly up to Ensenada and get things straightened out.

So at daylight, Tuesday, Francisco headed north to try and get the red tape untangled and Bob, Pete and I set out in the helicopter for the site of the wrecked airplane, intending to fly over some of the palm-studded canyons on the way. Munoz and Jean were to join us at noon at a little landing strip Munoz had found and explored not too far from the palm-lined canyons.

Munoz insisted he could land and take off from this strip, provided he was flying light with the least possible load.

However, it was a short, rough airstrip and while at the time I didn't have misgivings, later on I had plenty of them.

So Bob, Pete and I left the Hamilton Ranch and started flying on a compass course for our objective.

We went over some wild, rough country and then much to my surprise came to a little house, a corral and even a little stretch of barbed wire fence out in the middle of hills where there was no road, no well-defined trail; in short no evidences of civilization and no reason for a ranch to be there.

We circled around looking the place over and I wish now we had landed. Apparently there was no one home, so we kept on our way, and after a while came to the first of the palm trees.

The palm trees began in a rolling country where the canyons were not deep but were little more than valleys. Then gradually as we progressed south and east the valleys became canyons and the canyons became a little deeper and the walls more abrupt. Here the palm trees grew in greater abundance.

It was quite evident that there was water in these canyons and that there were many, many canyons.

We saw trails going to the water holes in places, but whether these were trails made by game, by wild burros or cattle we had no means of knowing. We saw no living thing in the country, although there was unquestioned evidence that the country was full of wild life.

The sand in the washes was liberally dotted with coyote tracks, rabbit tracks, deer tracks, and there were well-defined trails which had undoubtedly been made by deer, but the sun was now well up and the animals were all under cover.

As we continued flying toward the mountains, the canyons became deeper and deeper. The canyon walls were more abrupt and there was more and more evidence of water and of palm trees.

Here is a section of Baja California which is in all probability absolutely unknown except to a few ranchers. It has also, perhaps, been visited by prospectors from time to time.

I feel reasonably certain that there are parts of this country my friend Goldbaum had explored and of which he had shown me photographs many years ago. But it is a country no writer has ever described to my knowledge and as far as the tourist is concerned, it is nonexistent.

Rough, rugged, palm-lined canyons with great water holes in the rock would open up into little valleys covered with palm, mesquite and various types of desert vegetation. The sandy washes were literally covered with game tracks and there was cool shade, an abundance of water and marvelous scenery. There were, however, no signs of human beings, no human habitations, apparently no means of communication with any of the roads.

We hopped around exploring the canyons briefly and then went on up to the high mesa country looking for the wrecked airplane.

And we couldn't find it.

It was one of the most embarrassing experiences I have had in a long time. I had flown over that plane several times. I thought I knew the country as well as the proverbial palm of my hand, but after I got there the country all looked the same. I found dozens of places which looked exactly like the place where the airplane was, the only difficulty was the airplane wasn't there.

So eventually, as it was approaching the hour when we were to meet Jean and Munoz at the landing strip, we started back, taking time out to explore some of the canyons that we had previously flown over with Munoz.

A most challenging circular mark we had seen in the

bottom of one of the canyons, and which had variously been interpreted as a corral, a cavern, or a natural depression, turned out to be a little of all three.

A cap of hard granite rock had crossed over the watercourse, causing a waterfall which in turn had resulted in a big circular depression, running back well under the hard granite.

Here there were evidences of civilization because someone had put a fence across the lower part of this depression to make a species of corral out of it, but there was no clue as to who had done it or why it had been done, or how long ago.

Occasionally we ran onto a few cattle that looked as though they belonged to someone, and up in some of the wilder country we encountered cattle that undoubtedly had reverted to a wild state. They were completely "bronco" living in virtually inaccessible terrain where it would have been a sheer impossibility to have put on anything like a profitable cattle drive.

But some of the "tame" cattle in the lower reaches of the canyons and this rude corral, which had been made out of the cavern beneath the cap stone, indicated that there were *vaqueros* who worked the lower and more accessible parts of the canyon country.

Beyond that in the palm-lined canyons we found no indication of human beings.

So we hopped over a couple of ranges of mountains and descended to the little ranch with its landing strip where we were to meet Jean and Munoz.

They were already on the ground and had brought a good lunch which with cool water was very welcome indeed.

The rough strip on which Munoz had landed was pretty well grown up with vegetation which seemed insignificant from the air, but on the ground presented formidable obstacles which had to be avoided. Some of the vegetation had great wicked thorns which were fully capable of puncturing the tires of an airplane. So all of us pitched in with machetes and a short-handled shovel to try and make the landing strip a little safer for the take-off.

When we had finished, Jean and Pete stayed at the corral with the airplane while Francisco Munoz climbed into the helicopter with us to guide us back to where we could find the wrecked airplane.

Once more we went over a whole network of palm canyons with great pools filled with water carved into the granite, but since we now had a definite objective in mind we kept fairly well up in the air until we located the airplane. Then we came down, circled around it and finally landed.

Some Mexicans with burros had managed to get to the airplane. It had been quite thoroughly dismantled as far as anything of value was concerned, and sheets of aluminum had even been taken from the wings of the plane.

Francisco Munoz inspects the wreckage of the light airplane which was forced down. (The two occupants died of thirst.)

We land by a water hole.

While this plane was in rather an isolated country, knowing the country to the west as we did from our helicopter explorations we were not too surprised to find that someone had been in there with a pack string and probably secured enough from the wreckage to build a pretty good little cabin somewhere, the walls lined with sheet aluminum.

After looking around we started back for our landing strip and this time dropped down to inspect the canyons along the way until finally we decided to land in a particularly attractive canyon and see if we could find signs of human occupancy.

So we lowered the helicopter until we were only a few feet off the canyon floor, glided along between the abrupt walls until we came to a place where we wanted to land by a big water hole, and put the helicopter down on the sheer granite and shut off the engine.

We explored around for some time and found nothing to indicate any human being had ever been in that canyon.

So then we got back in the helicopter, flew on down a few miles and again came down to explore the tracks in the sand.

As we had surmised from the air, there were numerous deer tracks, some cat tracks, coyote tracks, rabbit tracks, the tracks of quail and of dove.

Here again we found no link with civilization.

So we went on back to the landing strip. Munoz and Jean got into the plane, and Pete, Bob and I climbed back in the helicopter.

I watched with my heart in my mouth as Munoz took off on that landing strip.

From our vantage point in the helicopter poised a couple of hundred feet above the landing strip, we could see the whole procedure, and as Munoz started lifting the plane into the air I felt certain that he wasn't going to make it.

As Munoz explained to me later, on a short landing strip it is always advisable to take advantage of all the landing

Munoz takes off from a Baja California road.

We make rendezvous with pilot Francisco Munoz and the pickups
loaded with gasoline.

strip there is. Some people, he explained, get nervous and
try to use only half or three-quarters of the strip. Munoz
takes it all.

However, Munoz got safely in the air, and we started
back toward the Hamilton Ranch looking for the pickups
since Munoz had managed after his early morning flight to
Ensenada to get the necessary procedures "expedited."

Munoz would fly on ahead, keeping in touch with us by
radio. Eventually he found the pickups far to the north of
where our schedule called for. It turned out they had had
even more delays after they got on the road, and what with
having fought their way over rutty, bumpy, washboarded
and dusty roads, they were in no mood to be argued with by
someone who came drifting down from a helicopter and insisted, "The roads are good. We've been looking at them from
the air."

However, that's one of the penalties a person pays for
not keeping up to schedule and so it gave me a great deal of
pleasure to point out to them scornfully that we had flown
over all of the roads they had traversed and there was

Munoz and Jean take off from a dangerous air strip.

Munoz and Jean just clearing trees after take-off.

nothing on earth to keep them from being at least three hours ahead of where they were.

The others controlled their homicidal impulses with an effort, and went on to make camp while Munoz, Jean, Pete, Bob and I went back to the Hamilton Ranch to spend the night.

The next day we tried to make it up to the fellows who had been slogging their way down the road. I landed from the helicopter and took over one of the pickups. Pete took over one of the other pickups and the others took turns in the helicopter exploring the canyons they had seen from the air when flying with Munoz on those first trips of aerial reconnaissance. They gently descended into the canyons, landing by deep water holes where Emery even went so far as to take a swim.

That night we were to make camp up in the granite country. Munoz took off late in the afternoon to get Jean back to the ranch, to pick up some important mail for me, and to bring one of the other secretaries back down to join the party.

The author leaves the helicopter to confer with the other members of the party.

#8

We Tackle the Canyons Again

The next day we started our caravan south with Pete Rivas taking over the job of driving one of the pickups. Sam, Bob and I got in the helicopter to start exploring in earnest.

We first flew down to the old mission of Santa Maria, a mission which as yet has no road to it.

An interesting and enterprising rancher at Cataviña is slowly and laboriously building a jeep road down to it, but since he is working under considerable difficulties and without the aid of machinery, it is a pretty rough job. At this time the road was still some three miles from the mission itself.

The plans for this road are most ambitious. The rancher wants to follow the old trail from the mission all the way down to the Bay of Gonzaga.

We wanted to see just what the new road was like, survey the old trail, and take a look at some canyons back of the old mission. So we started out with cameras, films and high ambition. We had a full day planned.

We reached Santa Maria Mission without difficulty and Bob put the helicopter down in front of the ruins. We took some photographs, and then went back up in the air gaining some elevation so we could determine just where we wanted to go next.

Sam thought there were interesting canyons to the south of the mission; I thought there were interesting canyons to the north; and for the purpose of clarifying the issue Bob put the helicopter pretty well up in the air.

It was this that saved us.

Suddenly and without the slightest warning a wall of wind hit us that attained a speed, as we afterwards learned, of ninety miles an hour.

Our helicopter was heavily loaded for a day of exploration, with a full supply of gas in the main tank and two auxiliary tanks, which could be attached to the aircraft also loaded to the brim. In addition to that we had our survival kit, some repair tools in case we had to use them and had the side racks attached to the runners. Taken by and large our top air speed was cut down by at least twenty-five miles an hour.

This wind picked us up as though it had been a giant hand, shook us as a terrier shakes a rat and then started hurling us down to the south and out toward the gulf.

Bob saw that it was useless trying to buck that wind at the higher elevations and went down lower to see what could be done.

Down low we had no difficulty measuring the velocity of the wind. We found out how fast it was moving by the simple expedient of turning the helicopter into the wind just above the ground and watching the airspeed indicator.

At a time when the air speed indicator was showing fifty-five miles an hour, the helicopter was standing perfectly still.

So we "hit the deck" and started looking for one of the passes which led through the mountains and up to the country of Dry Lake Chapala (Laguna Seca Chapala).

As we got into the rough terrain at the point where the road entered the pass, we encountered terrific turbulence, and it was of such a degree as to be well calculated to frighten anyone.

At times that helicopter would be hit by a wall of wind and sent spinning up in the air, only to have a gust swirling around the mountain catch it like an avalanche of snow coming off a steep mountainside and beat it down toward the ground.

We made two efforts to get through passes and couldn't make it because of the terrific turbulence.

Then we came to the last pass between the really high mountains and the lake.

I don't know what would have happened if we hadn't made this pass. I was afraid to ask at the time and I haven't cared to ask since, because we made it. But Bob confided to us afterwards that he was giving the helicopter one hundred per cent power as we entered this pass — something which is almost never done with this particular model.

In fact it's possible to take a heavy load and rise straight up from the ground like a shot, using only sixty per cent of power. But here Bob was using every bit of power he had. There just wasn't any more.

I have never ceased to marvel at the maneuverability of that machine or at Bobs' skill as a pilot. While we could feel the turbulent air currents pushing and pulling, lifting and descending, Bob managed to keep the helicopter at a fairly uniform distance off the ground and away from the canyon walls.

It was, however, an experience I wouldn't care to repeat.

Looking back on the experiences of that day, I begin

Helicopter at Mission Santa Maria.

The helicopter skims along the shore as we approach the bay.

to realize why the helicopter companies hestitated when I suggested they charter a helicopter to explore Baja California.

When we finally got well into this pass we were not more than fifty or sixty feet from the wall of the mountain on the one hand, not over thirty or forty feet above the ground on the other hand. Moreover, Bob was giving the helicopter everything it had, and I felt like an egg yolk in a cake-mixing machine.

But we got through the worst of it, came to a point where Bob had some reserve power, and soon found ourselves on the other side of the high mountain range where the wind was still terrific but the turbulence had subsided somewhat. From this point we were able to get to Arturo Grosso's house on Lake Chapala, where we made a landing, shook hands with the genial Arturo, and went inside the house to have coffee and tortillas while we waited for our caravan to catch up.

They arrived about one o'clock and were mighty relieved to see us there. They had been experiencing terrific winds and the roads had given Pete all the Baja California driving that he ever wanted.

So after a brief conference it was decided that we'd take the helicopter on down to the Bahia de Los Angeles without doing any more exploring, and the caravan would try to make it in there that night.

Back in the helicopter with the wind behind us we went down that road at a hundred and fifty miles an hour and in such a short time that it seemed hardly possible, found ourselves coming into Bahia de Los Angeles. There we found the bay glistening in the sunlight, the air completely calm and not even the sign of a whitecap.

We landed, saluted Antero Diaz and then a surprised Juanito.

HOVERING OVER BAJA

Ynes, it turned out, was making a truck trip into Ensenada but was due back within twenty-four to forty-eight hours.

So we got in our cabins, made reservations for the rest of our party, knowing that they were going to be thoroughly tired when they arrived. Thinking of the punishment they were taking, I know that I felt somewhat guilty as I stretched out for a siesta — but slept soundly nevertheless.

The others arrived a little later than had been expected and were bone-weary from fighting the road. We had some liquid refreshment which was well calculated to change their entire outlook on life and after they had experienced a couple of jolts of that and a good dinner, they regarded the situation much more philosophically.

The next morning we started the caravan out for the dry lake country, a journey of some forty-odd miles most of it in four-wheel drive. It would take them nearly all day to make it.

They were not only going to make a base camp on the

Bob Boughton, Pete Rivas and Murl Emery in front of our cabins at Bahia de Los Angeles.

dry lake but were going to find a hard, smooth place and mark out a landing strip on which Munoz could land.

Munoz was due in that night with Peggy, one of my secretaries who was bringing the inevitable high-priority television scripts from the office. She would be accompanied by Dr. Westphal and his wife Lilie.

Those of you who have read *Neighborhood Frontiers* will remember Dr. Westphal as the devoted friend and family physician who had made a seven hundred and fifty mile drive to get Jean through an acute attack of influenza when we were making our trip into Mexico's barrancas. At that time Lilie was one of my secretaries who lived at my ranch and who went along on that trip, taking dictation on the manuscript of the book as we traveled.

Westphal, then a widower, had subsequently taken an interest in my personal health, which I found most flattering.

I rang up Westphal one night (it's about thirty miles from his office in Elsinore to my ranch) and said "Look, Doctor, I've got a little tickling sensation in my throat which usually means I'm starting to take a cold, and a cold would raise the deuce with me at this time because I'm going to have to do a lot of dictation tonight and tomorrow.

"It's about five o'clock now and if you'll telephone a prescription over to the drug store, I'll have Sam get it before the store closes."

Westphal said "Erle, I'll be down there within thirty minutes."

I said, "For heaven's sakes, Doctor, it's not *that* important. Just give me something for my throat and . . ."

"You look here, Erle Gardner," he interrupted, "I don't tell you how to write mystery stories and you're not going to tell me how to practice medicine. I'll be down there within thirty minutes."

And within thirty minutes there he was. He gave me medicine for my throat. He gave me medicine for my sinuses. He gave me antibiotics. He took my blood pressure. He looked at my throat. He went up to the main house and had dinner and stayed there during the evening, coming down about every hour and a half to see how I was getting along.

I was up to my ears in an emergency matter which required pouring words into the dictating machine and it wasn't until midnight that I decided to roll in and take a much-needed rest.

Dr. Westphal was still there looking after me.

It wasn't until some months later when he had married Lilie that I began to entertain a deep-seated suspicion.

I wanted to make a test.

"Look here," I said to Jean, "ring up Dr. Westphal. Tell him that I've just been bucked off a horse and hit my head on a rock; that blood is oozing out of one ear; that I'm seeing double; and that I'm coughing up a little blood.

"I'll bet you twenty dollars that he says, 'Tell him to take two aspirins and go to bed and if he isn't better in the morning have Sam bring him into the office.'"

Jean wouldn't make the call. She said it was ridiculous. That Westphal would burn up the roads getting there. She didn't even think the idea was funny. Perhaps it wasn't, but I thought so at the time and since it was good for a laugh in a world where laughs are all too few, the idea served its purpose.

Because Westphal is one doctor who can't regard his patients impersonally but who considers each and every one as a member of his family, suffers when they suffer and when they are faced with some incurable disease gets all broken up himself, the guy is continually overworked and weighted down with responsibilities.

Dr. Westphal.

He had seen some of my colored pictures of the palm-lined canyons and I knew that he would give a great deal for a Mexican adventure, but under the circumstances the time element made it virtually impossible for him to get away.

The thought that I could give Dr. Westphal an opportunity to see these canyons at firsthand¹ was intriguing. I knew that his commitments were such that he couldn't

Coming in for a landing at the dry lake after we had moved most of
the duffel over into the canyon.

possibly make the trip except over a weekend in an airplane, and when it turned out our schedule would enable
us to fly down over a weekend, I was as the expression
goes, "tickled pink."

So while we were planning this helicopter trip I invited Dr. Westphal to come down and suggested to him
that in view of the fact I was going to have Munoz flying
back and forth bringing mail and television scripts, if he
could arrange to get a Friday and Saturday off he could
make the trip down with Munoz, come into camp in one
of the palm-lined canyons in the helicopter and then return Sunday with Munoz so that he could be in his office
Monday morning. Westphal's eyes lit up. His voice had a
note of enthusiasm I hadn't heard since he had told me
over the phone he would be at my ranch within thirty minutes to take care of my sore throat.

While we were waiting for the machines to get in place
in the dry lake and a base camp to be established, and since

178

Munoz, Peggy, Westphal and Lilie weren't due to arrive until afternoon, Bob and I decided it might be a good plan to explore some of the very rugged mountains to the south of Bahia de Los Angeles and see if we couldn't perhaps get a look at some of the bighorn mountain sheep which are supposed to be rather plentiful in the area.

So we left Pete there at Bahia de Los Angeles, got Antero Diaz in the helicopter to guide us and took off on a trip of exploration.

I had also been asking Bob Boughton if it would be practical to take a helicopter up into a section of mountain territory where it was impossible for any human being to travel (except with the aid of ropes and regular mountain-climbing equipment), to land on some inaccessible ledge, and then go out and walk around on whatever ground was available for walking, returning to the helicopter and on to some other ridge.

Bob assured me that it was perfectly feasible and promised a demonstration.

So with a crowd watching us at Bahia de Los Angeles we shot straight up in the helicopter, poised for a moment over the camp and then took off for the high mountains to the south and east.

Looking these mountains over I could well believe that no one had ever been in them — except perhaps some prospector who *might* have followed some of the more accessible ridges; but up in the higher places the mountains consisted of loose rock, of perpendicular ridges, of smooth material like sandstone, of tumbled boulders, and all in all a terrain that was exceptionally forbidding.

In exploring country of this sort it is hard to realize the difference which exists between flying in a plane at a low elevation on the one hand, and in getting down into the canyons with a helicopter so that one is moving along

Mountain sheep getting their first look at a human being.

within a few feet of the sheer cliffs on the other hand. It becomes possible in the latter instance to explore canyons where the walls come down on each side a seeming scant fifty feet from the sides of the helicopter.

We rounded a rough promontory and came on two mountain sheep who had been alerted by the sound of the motor and were looking about with startled curiosity.

As soon as they saw the helicopter they took off, running around the side of the mountain, and Bob immediately swung the helicopter off to one side and out over the canyon so as not to alarm them further.

The better class of helicopter pilots are very careful about chasing deer or similar game in rough country, fearing that the animals may become so panic-stricken when they realize they are being pursued that they will hurt themselves. It would be a horrible thing to leave some animal lying with a broken leg out on the side of a mountain.

However, I did get a quick picture of the animals running away from the helicopter along the steep slope.

We then went up another canyon and finally came to a narrow ridge perhaps fifty feet wide but with an almost straight drop on both sides and an imposing view of the country.

Bob landed here to show how easy it would be to go out sheep hunting in a helicopter, land in some remotely inaccessible place and start hunting operations from there.

I got out of the helicopter and walked the narrow ridge as far as I could go, trying to get a picture that would show the terrain, but there wasn't room enough for me to get into a position of vantage. I snapped a couple of pictures, but with a two dimensional camera it's quite difficult to look at these pictures and have any idea of the nature of the country either to the right or to the left.

We took off once more and went back in the general vicinity of the place where we had seen the sheep and suddenly came on two more sheep — or perhaps they were the same ones. I couldn't ask them their names.

These sheep showed no evidence of fear, only curiosity.

Bob lands the helicopter on a ridge; Antero looks around.

We land in a canyon.

They stood looking at the helicopter as we hovered over them. I was sitting there in plain sight and trying to talk to them, hoping that the sound of my voice as I assured them we only wanted to take their pictures would hold them steady.

The larger of the two sheep looked at us with speculative appraisal. The smaller one tried to hide behind a little bush, and it was surprising to see how he could blend with the scenery as soon as there were just a few branches to break the view.

We remained there within a few feet of the sheep. I could even see the eyelids of the animals as they regarded us. From the look of curiosity on the face of the large sheep and the manner in which he acted, I feel certain he had never seen a human being before.

We photographed these sheep for a while, then dropped down the steep slope, turned and twisted with the wind-

182

ings of the canyon until at length we came down to sea level and turned off in the grasses to see if we could jump a coyote.

We were successful within the first few seconds. This coyote took off at high speed in a straight line. We followed along taking pictures of him until it became apparent he was getting exhausted; his mouth was wide open, his flanks heaving with labored breathing. But during all of this time he kept running at top speed and in a straight line, doubtless feeling that he was being pursued by some super-eagle.

We left him so that he wouldn't become too exhausted and went back looking for another adventure, and within a couple of minutes located another coyote in marsh grass along the edge of the ocean.

This coyote acted entirely differently from the other. It would run only a few feet, looking back at the pursuing helicopter, then would dodge and double back, moving so rapidly that it was all but impossible to get a picture.

This coyote was thinking every minute of the time.

We next flew low along the beach, returning to the

We hover over a coyote who starts for other parts of Baja.

The helicopter hovers over the dry lake.

Bahia de Los Angeles, flying over a school of fish which was being "worked" by a flock of birds, watching what happened as some of the birds dove under the water and swam frantically underneath the surface.

Feeling we had perhaps saved the lives of countless anchovies, we kept on flying toward Bahia de Los Angeles and then came in to hover over the camp.

Antero Diaz was one very pleased individual. He picked up the microphone of the public address system on the helicopter and, as we hovered over the camp, told everyone of his exciting experiences, of the sheep he had seen, of the coyotes he had chased, and of the places he had been.

It was just too much.

In the minds of the people we hadn't been gone long enough to go anywhere, and as Antero Diaz related our adventures I fancied I could see a look of skepticism on some of the faces that were staring up at us.

We landed and had lunch, and then Munoz came in with Peggy, Lilie and Dr. Westphal.

We flew out to the dry lakes and inspected the camp which the fellows had located and which they were putting up as a permanent camp even as we landed. They had worked out a landing strip for Munoz' plane and everything was all fixed for an assault on the canyons.

That night we flew back to sleep at Bahia de Los Angeles while the others got things shipshape in camp and got the material arranged to be transported over into the Sal Si Puede Canyon. I had a feeling of great satisfaction. Tomorrow, I assured myself, there would be many adventures.

Those canyons had been a continuing challenge from the time I had first seen them from the air, and I know Emery had spent many a waking hour at night wondering how a person could use ingenuity, the inventions of a modern age and persistence in order to plumb their mysteries.

And now it looked as though we were going to master the secrets of those canyons.

We were out at the dry lake early the next morning. The helicopter picked up a load of camp equipment, took off over the rocky ridges for Sal Si Puede Canyon and a little exploration to locate a camp site.

The helicopter was back within thirty minutes having located a camp where there was water, shade and firewood.

It was necessary to dig down a few inches for the water and it had a peculiar taste, but was certainly all right for washing purposes and we could carry enough drinking water for our camp needs.

So the helicopter picked up another load of material, I climbed in, we arose from the ground and within a few minutes were drifting over the rough, boulder-encrusted moutain barrier and, almost before I realized it, we were over the coveted canyon, and were settling for a landing at the place where they were making camp.

We now had Juanito and Ynes with us and things took

The helicopter speedily returns for another load of camp supplies.

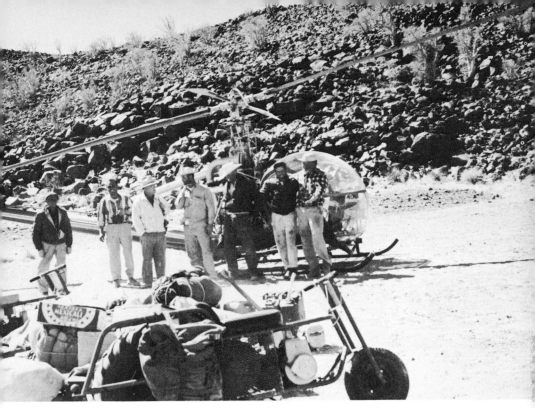

The personnel and duffel, which had to be moved by the helicopter, presented quite a problem.

shape very rapidly. A "spike" camp was established there in the canyon and the helicopter shuttled back and forth bringing in men and supplies.

We didn't as yet have the Pak-Jaks over there, but I couldn't wait, nor as it turned out could the others. We all started out on foot exploring the canyon, leaving Juanito and Ynes to get the camp set up while Sam and J. W. Black supervised getting the Pak-Jaks transported "over the hump," into the canyon and then tuned up for operation.

I hadn't gone very far before I realized why those canyons were unexplored.

Here it was the middle of February with much of the United States covered with snow and ice, while we were in a semi-tropical climate surrounded by palm trees and walking up country which had perhaps never known a

The helicopter bringing the Pak-Jaks into the canyon.

human foot within the memory of any living man — and
it was hot!

The sunlight was so intense and so highly actinic that
the needle on the exposure meter for my camera instantly
shot up to the highest reading. The sun came pouring down
from overhead and then was reflected back from the canyon walls as well as from the sandy floor of the canyon in
a blinding glare.

Because the air was dry the shadows seemed coal black
contrasting with the dazzling highlights. Between sunlight
and shadow there was that sharp line of demarcation which
I have seen so frequently on the desert and which is caused

by the fact the atmosphere is so free of moisture there is no diffusion of the sunlight.

I was of course tremendously excited. It was impossible to be otherwise.

Here were animal tracks all over the floor of the canyon. Some of these tracks I could classify and some I couldn't.

For instance, I came on a place where water had been standing until it had recently evaporated leaving a dry, silty deposit, and in this silty deposit some huge animal with great claws had been either trying to catch something and had left the tracks of claws which had been raked across the silt, or had been perhaps trying to catch some animal in the water before the water had evaporated, and had left indistinct paw marks and great raking claw marks in the silt.

I found numerous bird tracks, cat tracks, fox tracks, mountain sheep tracks, deer tracks, and then a little fox ran out ahead of me, took one look and decided he didn't want any part of me, and drifted across the floor of the canyon with his tail all fluffed out.

This was an instinctive reaction. There was no chance whatever that fox had even seen a human being before.

Then Leo Roripaugh and I came on a covey of quail.

Here again were wild things that knew nothing of human beings. Quite evidently we puzzled those quail. They circled together in a compact group, each one voicing his opinion in the liquid gutturals of quail language.

After a while the big cock quail that had assumed a position of leadership decided the flock had better get out of there, so they flew briefly some twenty or thirty yards.

I thought it would be interesting to see how quickly these quail reacted to being pursued — it is pretty generally conceded that what makes animals wild is not so much being shot at as being pursued by hunters.

The helicopter brings me back to camp and hovers for a moment over

So Leo and I started following them to see how close we could get to them for the second time and a third time.

After about the second encounter, those quail were just as wild as any quail I have ever seen in the United States. They simply didn't want any part of us and they took one more flight and disappeared.

We searched that darn canyon and every clump of brush in it up one side and down the other and we couldn't get a trace of those quail.

So we went back and resumed our explorations. I personally had had so much excitement in one day that I was emotionally weary. Just as the man whose legs have had all the walking he can take in the course of a day hates the idea of getting up and climbing a flight of stairs, so when my eyes would fix on something interesting I just didn't want it to pan out. I didn't want any more excitement that day.

I finally sat down in the shade of a palm tree and it came to me that it was a long, long way to walk back. I realized that I was feeling the heat, that although the air was so dry there was no sense of perspiration, my body

the place where the men are waiting to unload the Pak-Jaks.

had been perspiring profusely but the moisture had evaporated just as soon as the air touched it.

I was just plain good and tired — bushed, all in, hot and dehydrated.

And then I heard a welcome sound: The helicopter was coming up the canyon looking for us. Bob hovered overhead and then came to a landing within fifty feet of where I was standing. He opened the door of the plastic bubble and said casually, "Get in and I'll take you back to camp."

Oh welcome words!

I got in the helicopter and a second later was hovering over the tops of the palm trees, then gliding down the canyon, and within a few minutes was back in the welcome shade of camp, a camp which had now become pretty well fixed up, with a little fireplace flanked by boxes containing pots, pans and provisions. Our sleeping bags had been deposited in a pile, and, using one of these sleeping bags as a backrest, I settled in the shade and was almost immediately dozing, half conscious of my surroundings, half wrapped in refreshing slumber.

The helicopter, loaded with three passengers and two Pak-Jaks, comes in for a landing.

Sam and J. W. got the Pak-Jaks running and after a while we did some motorized exploration down the canyon.

It soon became apparent that despite the fact we had managed to get into the canyon and establish a base camp, we hadn't conquered the canyon by any manner of means. In fact it was inevitable that the canyon was going to conquer us because there was simply too much canyon to be explored within anything like the time we could give to exploration.

Every cave we found that was big enough for human habitation had the unmistakable marks of prehistoric fires. Ever so often there were interesting side canyons a little too rocky to pay us to ride the Pak-Jaks up them, but studded with palms and potentially even more interesting than the main canyon. And we knew that it would be up these side canyons that we would be more apt to find the remains of prehistoric Indian settlements.

The country was interlaced with veins of lighter colored material running through the granite and in places there were quartz veins in plain sight, some of them too far up the almost perpendicular walls to be reached without the aid of ropes and professional mountain-climbing equipment, but some of them were where it was possible to climb up and get samples.

And it is interesting that we came out of that canyon without a single mineral sample. We were simply too busy doing other things to waste time with prospecting.

By nightfall we were all good and weary. We tumbled into our sleeping bags and I doubt very much if anyone was bothered by insomnia. I felt as if I had been drugged.

The next morning I tackled a television script which Munoz had brought with him, and using my portable dictating machine made a whole series of comments con-

The author uses his portable dictating machine to record some interesting data on the canyon.

cerning our explorations of the canyons and the wild life we had seen.

Then I tackled some of the important correspondence Peggy had brought and shortly before noon was pretty well caught up with emergency matters.

Quite a wind was blowing at this time and it began to look as if we might have a problem with turbulence later on in the day.

Munoz was going to fly the Westphals and Peggy back to Tijuana that day and I could see that he was looking at the weather with just a bit of concern, so it was finally decided they would start a little earlier than intended.

Bob Boughton ferried them across the hump in two loads and then shortly after his second return, we heard the roar of the motor on Munoz' airplane, and he flew up over the canyon headed for Tijuana, bucking a headwind which, as we afterward learned, attained velocities of eighty-five to ninety miles an hour.

Back in camp we settled down for a little rest and waited for the wind to go down.

Sam, J. W. Black and Leo Roripaugh, restless individuals filled with energy and enthusiasm, were off on Pak-Jaks exploring the country.

Emery and I sat watching the palm fronds whipped by the wind and trying to reassure each other that the wind would go down within an hour or two. However, I think we both remembered our previous experience with the wind on the ocean when we had sat there trying to wait out the storm.

Sometime early in the afternoon Bob Boughton announced that while the wind didn't seem to be going down he didn't think it was getting any worse and if he didn't have such a heavy load of extras he felt that we could have a fairly comfortable trip of exploration.

So Emery and I jumped in the helicopter and we took off exploring the canyons.

It was windy all right, and there was considerable turbulence; but we explored those canyons from the height of the palm trees up one side and down the other.

With the helicopter not over forty or fifty feet above the fronds of the palms we followed the Sal Si Puede up to the mountains, then hopped over to La Asamblea and went down it to the ocean.

At that level there was quite a bit of turbulence and I didn't take very many pictures — an oversight for which I have been kicking myself ever since. I had the cameras and the films, but I kept thinking that we would have smoother flights later on and at the time I just didn't realize how extensive those canyons were.

After we had explored the canyons to the point where they came into the big wash some five miles above the beach,

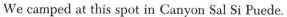

We camped at this spot in Canyon Sal Si Puede.

The canyons end at the ocean.

we flew on down to the beach, then took some time exploring the interesting highly colored cliffs by the wash. And so finally flew up the canyon and back to camp.

Black, Sam and Leo had by this time come to the conclusion there was a lot more canyon country than they had at first realized, and they wanted to ride the Pak-Jak down Sal Si Puede to reach the point where we had turned back on our last trip. They thought it was a matter of only three or four miles. When Emery and I had surveyed it from the air we also felt that it couldn't be much more than that. Actually, it turned out to be about eight miles of winding, twisting, sandy wash.

However, we started out on Pak-Jaks and rode down some three or four miles until we came to a large cave which stretched back some distance into the mountain and gave unmistakable signs of human occupancy.

Emery wanted to dig in that cave; Sam, J. W. and Leo

Palms in Sal Si Puede.

Camp in Sal Si Puede from the helicopter.

We cruise over the canyon, just above the tops of the palm trees.

wanted to go on down to the point where we had turned back on our previous expedition; and I decided that I would start walking back the three or four miles to camp just looking the country over.

I had a wonderful afternoon. I again encountered quail and this time made up my mind I would see what happened when they disappeared. I used infinite patience and then made the discovery that they didn't fly away at all. They simply started walking up the tumbled rocks of the mountain, moving slowly but steadily up out of the canyon.

Why quail should do this is more than I know. But that was their ace in the hole. It was their secret of protection. They walked quietly but steadily, covering quite a bit of ground and simply taking themselves up out of the canyon until finally they got so far up I could no longer see them distinctly.

Evidently they were from time to time pursued in that canyon by something that made this type of defensive tactics the only practical means of escape.

It could hardly have been any four-legged animal because then they could have resorted to flight. It must have been something in the nature of a hawk or an eagle which delighted to feed on quail, and by keeping on the ground and up in the jagged, tumbled rocks, they had a semi-subterranean line of escape which baffled whatever it was that was pursuing them.

I finally arrived in camp good and tired and after a while the others got in. We had dinner and then again the subject came up of the burning palm trees.

Just how dry and explosive were those palm trees anyway?

There was a dead palm a couple of hundred yards down the canyon which had lost its top and all semblance of life, but still clung to the skirts, or rather the skirts still clung to the palm. It was a stunted, dwarfed palm, not over some twenty feet high, but at least it would give us an opportunity to see just how combustible these palm skirts were.

We touched a match to this skirt and almost instantly the tree was enveloped in smoke which swirled up through the dried skirt just as though the dried palm leaves had formed a circular chimney — which was just about what they did.

A split second later the smoke was followed by flame and then almost before one could realize what was happening the palm tree was wrapped in flames, the wind giving the sheet of fire a circular motion so that the palm tree became a vortex of roaring fire and these flames shot high up into the air, many times the height of the tree.

As I said before, the palm leaves, when they get hot, emit some highly combustible gas, and not only would the

Burning palm.

flames shoot up in the air several times the height of the palm itself but high above these flames suddenly some pocket of gas would explode into flame.

It was one of the most spectacular fire exhibits I have ever seen, and the fact that the entire camp watched with breathless, astounded silence is perhaps the best way in which I can describe the effect. We were simply speechless. We had never expected any such spectacle.

The swirling flames continued for many minutes. It must have been perhaps ten or fifteen minutes in all, and then embers wrapped the dead trunk of the palm tree and the base of the tree for more than an hour.

Having started something like that it was hard to stop. We had fired our first palm tree in the interests of scientific research. Promptly, the others suggested that we would wait until it got dark and then do a little more "scientific research" to see what would happen.

What happened in the dark with the second palm tree was so breath-takingly spectacular that there were those in the party who wanted to carry on the "scientific research" to see what would happen if we burned a really big palm tree — those that we had been burning were not more than a quarter the size of some of the large ones.

However, after more sober thought we put our official stamp of disapproval on any more "scientific investigation" conducted with matches.

It is, however, plain to be seen why many of the Mexican prospectors must have treated themselves to an evening of fiery entertainment and this undoubtedly accounts for many of the burnt palms in the more accessible areas.

Later on that night, I made the mistake of bringing out the pocket calendar which I had taken with me.

#9

Problems of Further Exploration

A calendar is a remarkable instrument. We are inclined to take it for granted. Each December various firms issue complimentary calendars adorned with pictures of horses, nude women, beautiful scenery, all reproduced in vivid colors bearing advertising slogans and twelve detachable tags which mark the days of the coming year.

Probably no one stops to think what that calendar really means.

The Book of Nature is one of the most deceptive books ever printed. It is as if the Deity wanted to convince us that the evidence of our senses has no real validity.

When man tries to measure infinity by the yardstick of his infinite mind, he invariably comes to grief.

His eyes assure him that the world is flat. He knows that the sun rises in the east and sets in the west because he can see it do so every day. He knows that the stars revolve around the world because he can see them doing so, and when man wants to make a calendar he has nature's own pendulum, the phases of the moon, to guide him.

How many times primitive man must have wondered what was wrong as his wisest men tried to determine the passage of time and the length of the year.

Man needed to know the length of the year because he needed to plant crops. He needed to take advantage of the seasons, but there was no way he could get an accurate measurement of the year. There was no way he could predict the arrival of the seasons. The problem was so cunningly designed to baffle mankind that it wasn't even possible to get a fixed number of days in the year. There was an inevitable fraction.

The Mayan civilization was founded in large part upon the fact that its wise men did determine the length of the year. They knew when crops had to be planted. They knew when the rains were due. They knew when the year began and they knew when the year ended. And Mexico is enormously proud of its calendar stone which was the first accurate determination of the length of the year reached and perpetually recorded on stone. The calendar stone gives positive proof that one cannot understand the intricacies of nature and the problem of existence unless he first discards the evidence of his senses and disciplines his mind to accept the dictates of reason — and perhaps of pure faith.

But on a trip such as we were making, the calendar can be one of the most diabolical of all inventions.

When we had left home I had felt that two weeks with a helicopter would give us ample leisure to do everything we wanted. We could explore the canyons. We could look for old ruins. We could visit the site of wrecked airplanes and perhaps still make some interesting discoveries. We could prospect interesting outcroppings.

Exploring.

But I reckoned without the inexorable facts of life as disclosed by the calendar.

Actually it turned out we could do no such thing.

The helicopter was invaluable when it came to transporting provisions and material over the hump. It was a wonderful instrument to use in exploration and in making a map of the canyons so that we could find out what were the main canyons and what were the tributaries and how far they went. It had proven to be the key to a number of most interesting adventures.

On the other hand, the helicopter could only carry enough gasoline for limited cruising. It couldn't carry all

The helicopter relayed our stuff into a canyon camp.

our personnel and camping equipment over long distances. It was dependent upon pickups and our existence in turn depended upon the things that could be carried in the pickups: gasoline, drinking water, provisions, tents, sleeping bags, cameras, films and all the various and diverse things that are needed while living in the open.

The transportation of those things in four-wheel drive trucks was very much of a problem. It was possible to make perhaps a hundred miles a day over the rough main roads of Baja California, but when it came to the side roads and establishing camps within a reasonable distance of where we wanted to make our headquarters, we were faced with an entirely different problem.

We wanted to go again to the old mission of Santa Maria. We wanted to camp at the end of the road and explore that trail which we had seen from the air; a trail which had evidently been used to supply the mission from

We ride double on the Pak-Jaks.

the Bay of Gonzaga on the gulf side, a distance of perhaps twenty miles or so in an air line.

From the air this trail was a most interesting sight. It had been carefully laid out and all of the rocks along it had been pushed to the side of the trail, forming a boundary of rocks on each side (an interesting marker of all the old trails in Baja California).

Not only were the rocks taken from the trail but the boundaries they formed provided such sharp contrast with the beaten path that even on starlit but moonless nights it would have been possible to follow the trail.

Heavens knows whether this was the reason for combing the rocks from the trail and accurately delineating each side of the trail. It must have been for some similar purpose. In any event it was done. The rocks were moved and placed at regular distances outlining the trail.

We wanted to use our Pak-Jaks to explore that trail

from the mission all the way down to the Bay of Gonzaga. This trail had seen an enormous amount of use. A couple of hundred years ago, hundreds of thousands of steps by bare feet had worn that trail down through the solid rock, across the drifting sand from the mountains, to the bay where small boats could find a sheltered anchorage. But within the last hundred years it was quite possible that a person could count on the fingers of one hand the explorers who had actually traversed that trail — in fact as far as we could ascertain no one had traveled it.

Moreover, we wanted to explore some country to the west of Puertecitos where Francisco Munoz had from time to time and from a high elevation shown us what seemed to be the roofs of two huge buildings: arched roofs, with very definite indications that there was water in the vicinity. And people would laugh when anyone mentioned the possibility of water being in these dry, barren hills.

There were also palm-lined canyons in the vicinity of the Santa Maria Mission which no one knew anything about.

In addition to all of this we had some private objectives of our own.

Years ago Juanito and a companion, prospecting in a wash below Puertecitos where they were trying to find gold, had decided to sink a shaft at a place where they thought an ancient well might have been excavated. In fact there was the possibility that this was the scene of some old and very rich mine or perhaps a burial place for pirate treasure.

Juanito and his partner had come upon the bones of a man who had evidently been slain there by having his head cut open with some heavy, sharp instrument, perhaps a saber, perhaps the edge of a shovel.

In any event they had started excavating where they thought the well might have been located and soon dug into a circular hole which had been lined with cut stone. They excavated this to a distance of thirty feet where they encountered good drinking water and were never able to continue their excavations below the water line.

Juanito said he could guide us to this place and we wanted to explore it.

Now it was one thing to get the helicopter into these places, but quite another thing to get the helicopter *and* the supplies into those places.

Moreover, I personally had had my fill of trying to fight my way through the turbulent canyons of Baja California during periods of high wind — and we had to face the fact that at this season of the year it was quite possible we would encounter high winds which would be almost certain to last for three successive days and might well last longer.

A look at the map of Baja California, an estimation of distances, an examination of the problems of logistics as far as gasoline was concerned, and the problem of getting our four-wheel trucks spotted where we wanted them, was something which caused the days of the calendar to dissolve like a lump of sugar dropped into a cup of hot coffee.

I simply couldn't believe the facts as we started marshaling them and by the simple process of addition and subtraction arriving at certain mathematically accurate but unwelcome answers.

It now became apparent that a person could take three to four weeks exploring those canyons with Pak-Jaks and still have only a rudimentary idea of all of the various things that were in them.

Emery had done a little excavation in the Indian cave and had brought back some very interesting objects that had been buried some four feet below the surface of the ground among ashes and wind-blown dust which had con-

We stop our Pak-Jaks in front of the entrance to an Indian cave, which stretches back into the sheer rock.

stituted the floor of the cave some two hundred years ago. Because of the dry air these things were in a state of perfect preservation.

For one thing he had a fraction of a fishing net cunningly constructed from palm fronds. For another he had a small line which in all probability had been used as a fish line. It was made from fibers of plants, perhaps from the roots of palms. It had been so skillfully braided that it was thin but strong and there had been a knot worked into one end of it so that the loop in the knot was a complete part of the cord, somewhat the way the expert archer of today makes a loop in his bowstring.

We had seen more caves we wanted to explore, outcroppings of quartz we would like to look at, side canyons that were clamoring for exploration. We had seen a ledge with partially obliterated Indian writings and, of course, we had the urge to look around where Emery had found that old prospector's pick, because by this time we had the story of the dead prospector, the rattlesnake, the sack of rich ore, and knew that somewhere within a relatively short distance of the place where Emery had found that prospector's pick there must be an outcropping very rich in gold; perhaps a vein that had enough value to make what is known as "jewelry rock."

But to break up our spike camp, get things transferred back to the dry lakes, then get them loaded in the pickups, then get the pickups back to Bahia de Los Angeles so we could replenish the supplies of gasoline, then get the pickups back up the long road through Lake Chapala and down to Cataviña, then over the hand-constructed road toward the mission, another camp established and then to start explorations with the helicopter, all ate into the remaining days on the calendar.

It now became apparent that the delay in Ensenada while the trucks had been held up by the fiesta waiting to get the necessary clearance papers for personnel and the delay incident to that terrific windstorm we had encountered the day we first landed at Santa Maria Mission, had cut into our schedule more than we had realized. In fact we simply hadn't worked out an intelligent schedule. We had thought in terms of getting into those canyons, establishing a spike camp and traversing the canyons with Pak-Jaks, and our other thinking had been hazy. Exploring by helicopter would be easy. Two weeks with a helicopter? We'd cover hundreds of miles.

That much of our thinking had been all right, but the problem of transporting personnel, supplies and pickups over rough, four-wheel drive roads was the real determining factor.

Sam, J. W. and Leo had now closed the missing link. They had ridden the Pak-Jaks down the eight miles or so of canyon to a point where they had picked up the familiar

Murl Emery shows some of the artifacts he uncovered after digging
some four or five feet under the surface of the Indian cave.

landmarks indicating our point of greatest exploration on
the prior trip. Emery and I had been in the helicopter
when Bob piloted it up the Sal Si Puede Canyon to the
very end over the divide to La Asamblea and down the
entire length of La Asamblea to the mouth of the wash at
the ocean and then back up the wash to Sal Si Puede Canyon, and up Sal Si Puede Canyon to camp.

So we started chalking off the days of the calendar,
alloting activities for exploration and praying that we

J. W. Black and Sam Hicks return to camp from a trip of exploration.

wouldn't run into any really bad head winds because no matter how we handled things we had to have the helicopter loaded so heavily with personnel, auxiliary gas tanks and some emergency supplies and tools that we couldn't hope to get a speed of more than eighty or ninety miles an hour, if that, in calm weather; and of course if we encountered a few more ninety mile an hour head winds we would be using up all of our power standing still, even if we could keep out of the canyons where there was the terrific turbulence.

Even as we were making our plans the wind was howling overhead with such velocity that as we subsequently learned it had taken Munoz an extra hour and a half to get to Tijuana.

So we reluctantly decided that if the wind hadn't gone down by the next day we were going to have to break camp.

I went to sleep that night with mingled feelings. There was satifaction that we had to some extent conquered the problems of the canyon, but there was also the suspicion that the combined forces of the canyon and the calendar had conquered me.

The next day the wind was blowing again so we decided we had better move camp, get packed up and get started. And we knew it would represent an enormous amount of effort to accomplish all that and get the outfit back to Bahia de Los Angeles during daylight.

So again we started the long chore of getting all our material and all the various personnel back to the dry lake — and the wind started blowing with ever-increasing velocity.

By the time I got to the dry lake I found that dust and sand were blowing; the tent which had been put up to house our material that had been left behind was just on the point of blowing away; the wind had whipped the canvas until many of the stakes had been pulled out of the sand so many times that replacing them did no good.

At about this time Munoz returned from Tijuana with another one of my secretaries, Ruth ("Honey")* Moore, and her huband Walter and the inevitable television scripts and important mail.

So I took my portable dictating machine, moved off into the shelter of one of the pickups and again started the endless chore of dictating while the others got everything loaded into the pickups, and then I let the Moores ride into Bahia de Los Angeles in the helicopter so they could have the experience of a helicopter ride, while I got in with Munoz and we again made rendezvous at Bahia de Los Angeles.

---

* Everyone has called her Honey from the time she was knee-high to a grass-hopper so it has really become her name.

By working like Trojans the others managed to get the trucks in there that evening shortly after dark, and then the next morning they started loading up with gasoline and making plans to start up the road for camp at the end of the handmade road by the Santa Maria Mission.

A great deal depended upon what they found there in the way of conditions on the ground. If it was going to be exceedingly difficult to get the Pak-Jaks down over the rock-strewn mountains to the trail, we were going to have to give up exploring the trail as a part of the helicopter expedition, although the others would have time to make a hurried survey.

Leo Roripaugh had received some news which made it necessary for him to return to his ranch near Temecula and Sam Hicks had to be present for the wedding of his oldest daughter.

We had of course tried to make the entire trip at an earlier date but difficulties of getting everyone together, getting the helicopter on the job and arranging the charter appointments of Francisco Munoz so that we could count on him, made it necessary to fix dates in accordance with what we could do rather than what we wanted to do.

So it was apparent that Pete, Bob and I would have a day or two at Bahia de Los Angeles while we were waiting for camp to get established at the end of the hand-constructed road three miles more or less from Santa Maria Mission.

We decided to accept this delay philosophically and since Walter Moore decided he wanted to go north with the pickups and let his wife go on with the plane when it was ready to leave, we got Antero Diaz to take Honey, Bob Boughton, Pete Rivas and me on a fishing expedition and a pelican egg hunt.

The pelican is a huge bird and the eggs are about the

The pelicans have a total of three eggs.

We join Munoz for lunch.

size of turkey eggs. The quota is three per pelican and the
nests are made in sheltered canyons where the sun can per-
form most of the job of incubation; little canyons which
are sheltered from the wind but so situated that the sun
will give maximum service.

The manner of gathering pelican eggs is simple in the
extreme: You simply carry along a container filled with
fresh water. You pick the eggs out of the nest and drop
them into the container. If the egg sinks, it is edible. If it
floats, be very careful not to break it. Put it back on the
nest, because you are handling an embryo pelican encased
by a very thin and fragile shell.

That was an interesting adventure and I would have
enjoyed it even more if it hadn't been for the realization
that time was clicking remorselessly away.

When it became necessary for Munoz to fly north in
order to take Mrs. Moore back and get Sam home in time
for the wedding and Leo back to his ranch, we realized
that we had some further problems that required communication with the campers.

Since we were a restless lot and intensely impatient,
we instantly accepted Munoz' suggestion that he fly up to
locate the pickups and drop a note containing a revised
schedule in accordance with things I had learned over the
ship-to-shore telephone in calling the office from Bahia de
Los Angeles, and Honey, Bob Boughton and I decided to
fly up, look the situation over and deliver the note.

I wish now that we had had some two-way radio communication with the pickups. It would have been relatively
simple, if I had thought of it in time, to have arranged for
a portable radio in the pickups which could have picked up
the wave lengths of the radio on Munoz' plane, but that
was simply another thing we hadn't thought of.

Never again will I criticize the army for overlooking

Pink mountains at mouth of canyons.

Rugged mountains, narrow canyons.

things in the problem of logistics. The human mind (meaning my cranium) simply isn't capable of looking ahead and anticipating all of the problems which are going to arise in connection with a somewhat complicated expedition where it becomes necessary to synchronize the activities of a helicopter, an airplane, four four-wheel drive automobiles and the delivery of supplies, particularly when one throws in a family wedding, a weekly television show, an impatient book publisher, an overdue serial at *The Saturday Evening Post,* and the urgencies and emergencies which are the result of each day's incoming mail.

Flying north, Munoz took us over one of the highest peaks in Baja California and circled close to the side of the peak to show us where a DC-3 had come to grief several years before.

This twin-motored plane had been flying a cargo of live lobsters and some freight to the north. In addition there were nine passengers. It was heavy weather and the machine had come to grief on the very summit of the peak.

If the pilot had been fifty feet higher or if he had been a couple of hundred feet to one side, he would have missed the crash. Such is fate.

Munoz managed to fly quite close to the wreckage strewn along the side of the mountain, but since we intended to go back there by helicopter, land and make a closer inspection, Munoz, after a couple of passes, was on his way taking us over the Dry Lake Chapala and the ranch of Arturo Grosso, then on to Cataviña where the handmade road started that the rest of the party was going to take.

This road had now been completed for some eleven miles and we found that our party with the pickups had just arrived at the end of the road when we came flying over.

Taking picture of cliffs at mouth of canyon.

Since we had a note to drop, I prepared to launch it on its way.

Dropping a note from an airplane requires a little doing, particularly if the persons who are to receive the note are in rough country.

It is necessary to have some sort of a streamer on the container which will make the falling object readily visible and at the same time slow down its flight somewhat, and it is of course necessary to drop the note with due allowance for speed, wind resistance and distance so that it will come reasonably close to the persons for whom it is intended. In rough country a distance of a few hundred yards might well land the note in some inaccessible ravine or permit it to become concealed behind some massive boulder.

We had the note in a small cloth sack weighted with a rock. We had then tied a streamer of cloth to the sack.

In getting rid of the note it was necessary to throw it down with a hard motion so that the streamer wouldn't get entangled in the tail assembly of the plane.

I held the door of the plane partially open, bracing against the wind resistance while Munoz made a couple of passes over the pickups, then suddenly yelled, "Now!"

I threw the container down fast and hard, then released my pressure on the door of the plane and the wind resistance promptly slammed it shut.

The country was quite rough. There was some turbulence and Munoz was busily engaged in piloting the plane for the next few seconds so that we couldn't any of us make sure the others had received the note, but as we made another circle over the cars we saw the men clustered together as though reading a note. They gave us a go-ahead signal, so we took off, satisfied that our message had been received. Later on, there was some doubt, particularly on my part, because I had been so concerned the fluttering streamer might become entangled in the tail assembly that I had rolled it up pretty tight.

Since the note called for a rather complicated series of maneuvers and meetings, it would have been quite embarrassing if it hadn't been found. For instance, the air strip at Cataviña where Munoz had been planning to pick up Sam and Leo Roripaugh, had proven on a survey from the air to be too short for safety, so we had instructed Sam and Leo to go on over to the field at El Marmol where Munoz would pick them up on the following day.

It was true we had received a go-ahead signal from the men on the ground but did it mean "Go ahead and tell us what you want us to know," "Go ahead and drop the note," or did it mean "Okay we have the note"?

We kept on going north because Munoz wanted to show Bob the object he had sighted from high in the air which he thought might be the ruins of a big adobe building.

So we flew over the ghost city of El Marmol, site of the big onyx mine which had been operated for so many years by the Brown family. It was from this mine that virtually all of our ornamental onyx desk sets had originated.

While there are huge deposits of onyx here and it has for many years been quarried in huge slabs, shipped out for cutting and polishing into ash trays, pen and desk sets, etc., it finally became necessary to close the mine despite the fact that slabs of onyx are piled up awaiting shipment.

It is here that they built a schoolhouse of pure gem stone of the highest grade onyx. It is a beautiful structure, although the affluent atmosphere of gem rock contributes nothing to the ease with which pupils learn the three R's.

To the north and east of El Marmol the country becomes very tumbled and seemingly very barren, a succession of confused mountain ranges, long sandy washes, with only occasional patches of level ground. It is a country which is avoided by aviators wherever possible and when not possible, it is flown over at considerable height.

Flying at some ten or eleven thousand feet Munoz had frequently looked down on what seemed to him to be the ruins of large buildings. On at least one occasion he had caught the unmistakable glint of the sky being reflected from water. Since there was not supposed to be any water in this country, Munoz felt that his discovery indicated some artificial reservoir and had been eager to investigate and find out just what was below, but he was too cautious an aviator to lose altitude while flying unescorted over such terrain.

I had been with him on a couple of these trips when we had spent some time trying to puzzle out what was beneath. So now that we had the helicopter with us I was very anxious to get a close look.

On this present scouting trip, however, Munoz was flying at only about half the elevation that he maintained on his through flights and from this elevation as we came over the objects in question it looked as though they *might* be simply odd-shaped rocks which had been worn by water in such a way that the top of the largest rock looked like the arched roof of an adobe building.

Bob Boughton marked the place in his memory, and agreed that we would investigate it with helicopter, then Munoz turned the plane and we flew back to Bahia de Los Angeles arriving just as the sun was setting and the islands were turned to golden nuggets in a sea of deep blue.

#10

Lost Mission of Santa Ysabel

When we started out again with the helicopter we were intending to land on the peak at the site of the wreck of the DC-3. Munoz with his greater speed was going to fly his plane on ahead but would keep in constant touch with us by radio.

It soon became apparent that there was going to be quite a bit of wind and some turbulence. Munoz flying very high in order to avoid the turbulence became as solicitous about our welfare as a mother hen looking after her sole chick at a time when a hawk is circling overhead.

Bob Boughton's wife had flown down to join him at Bahia de Los Angeles and was with us in the helicopter, while Pete Rivas was flying with Munoz and was in charge of keeping in radio contact with us.

As the turbulence increased, Bob reluctantly decided it might be unwise to land on the mountain by the wreckage of the DC-3 but we could hover over it and get a pretty good view as well as some pictures.

So Bob relayed the information to Pete Rivas in Munoz' plane and told him to tell Francisco that we wouldn't try to land but would hover over the wreckage, then come through the pass and be over Lake Chapala at an estimated time.

Shortly after that message had been transmitted I looked down and saw a very well-defined trail which was of the sort that had been made to supply the old missions; so I asked Bob, after following that trail for two or three miles, if we couldn't go down to a lower elevation and take a look.

Bob obligingly put the helicopter down closer to the ground and in doing so lost radio communication with Munoz.

Following the trail for several miles we suddenly came upon some ruins, and as we hovered over those ruins taking a look at them it became apparent they were rather important ruins. This was not simply some old ranch house which had been abandoned. The construction had been elaborate and carefully executed. There was a graveyard with one very large white tomb and some smaller tombs. The structure had been built in at least two parts and in part on ground that had been leveled after first erecting a rock retaining wall and then laboriously filling the ground.

These were things which would hardly have been done in building an ordinary ranch house. Moreover, one could see no reason for the location of a ranch house in this particular locality.

We all knew of course of the famous Lost Mission of Santa Ysabel.

The stories of that mission are somewhat varied to suit the individual, but generally the legend is that when the

King of Spain ordered the evacuation of the territory by the Jesuits who had been in charge of the string of missions up and down the peninsula, the head of the Jesuits passed word that the priests were to surrender their missions peaceably and not to try to resist the order in any way; but that the missions were all the priests were to surrender, they weren't to turn over their treasure.

According to legend, the word went out that a new, hidden mission was to be constructed in an inaccessible place, and this was to be the storehouse of all the treasure that had been collected by the Jesuits. And, again according to rumor, this mission was constructed and was known as the Mission of Santa Ysabel. The location was kept secret, but it housed all of the wealth which had been accumulated by the Jesuit fathers.

When the time came for the Jesuits to evacuate, they were not exactly put under arrest but they were so closely supervised in their evacuation that they were able to carry nothing with them except the bare necessities of their personal wardrobe.

And so the legend of the Lost Mission of Santa Ysabel has gained strength over the years and the secret mission has been the object of much search.

The early mission fathers lived a life that was Spartan in its simplicity. There is considerable reason to doubt that they ever amassed any wealth, or whether they ever wanted any wealth. They were interested in building the missions, educating the Indians and in saving souls. They were not primarily interested in treasure hunting.

However, that was during a period when various Spanish military expeditions were diligently searching for gold. There were rumors of great treasure, so it is not surprising that the military authorities, having made certain that the Jesuits did not remove any treasure with them, would have expected

A section of the ruins of what may well be the Lost Mission of
Santa Ysabel.

that much gold had been left behind somewhere in a secret
storehouse.

Regardless of historical rumor and the probabilities that
the Jesuit priests had no treasure to hide, the fact remains
that it is distinctly possible the lost mission does exist, and
there are stories which have come down from the old Indians
indicating more or less definite locations.

It was, therefore, only natural that as we hovered over
these ruins and saw the extent of the ground that had been
leveled and realized the magnitude of the buildings, we
should become excited.

Under the circumstances there was only one thing to do
and that was to land. As Bob Boughton pointed out, however,
he was out of radio communication with Francisco and had
been for some time. Our last message had been to the effect
that we would be coming through the pass in the mountains
only about twenty minutes behind Munoz.

Nevertheless, we simply couldn't pass up this oppor-

226

tunity, so we put the helicopter down but realized that in fairness to Francisco and Pete we must make our stay exceedingly brief.

I would have given much to have had a full day to explore those ruins.

Someone had been living there rather recently. In fact it was quite possible that two people had been living there. Lean-tos had been constructed against the walls of the old ruins and it was evident that some prospector or explorer had spent some time there. It was also evident that this construction had taken place since the wreck of the DC-3, because aluminum which had been brought down from the wrecked airplane had been used in constructing these lean-tos.

It was also apparent that the main adobe building had been used as a ranch house for a good many years. Before the roof had caved in, some family or families had been living there. But that didn't answer the question of *when* the buildings were constructed and *why* they were constructed. We found evidence which was quite persuasive that the buildings had been constructed prior to the time they had been used as a ranch house and the construction had been part of a rather elaborate plan and carried out under the supervision of people who had considerable executive ability.

In short, during our brief stay we found nothing which indicated this could *not* be the Lost Mission of Santa Ysabel, but we found some things which indicated the strong probability that it *might* be the ruins of the lost mission.

In the meantime, as it turned out, Francisco was tremendously concerned about us. As the time passed with no word from us, Munoz insisted on turning back, and as it became apparent we had never come through the mountain pass, his concern mounted to such a point that Pete Rivas, who had unlimited confidence in the helicopter's ability to take care of itself under any conditions and over any terrain, started faking radio conversations and telling Munoz that he was in communication with us.

This reassured Munoz only briefly, as he soon detected suspicious flaws in Pete's improvisations and started a frantic search close to the ground looking for our wreckage. This in turn caused Pete considerable alarm, because neither the weather nor the terrain was conducive to low flying on the part of a fixed-wing airplane.

We cut our stay short, grabbed a few hurried pictures, climbed in the helicopter and shot straight up above the ruins, then started climbing up the mountains and finally got to a point where our radio signals reached Francisco's plane and Pete was able to let Francisco hear for himself that we were all right.

This caused tremendous relief on the part of Francisco. He knew that country, knew something of the turbulence and had become pretty well convinced we had encountered some major emergency.

So we both turned north again and flew on to the place where the pickups were camped. Munoz went on to make a landing at the strip at Cataviña, which he could do since he was now traveling light, and we put the helicopter down at the place where camp had been made.

It soon developed that while Sam and Leo had received our message all right that they were to go to the landing strip at El Marmol, they had decided to leave my Land Rover there instead of having one of the men come along to drive it back to camp. David Hurtado, who was spending some time at my ranch, was an expert driver and I had assumed he would take Sam and Leo to the air strip and return with the car so it would be available when camp was broken.

Bob Boughton rounds up the personnel by helicopter.

However, the car was now at the landing strip at El Marmol, there were only the pickups in camp and, as it turned out, the personnel was widely scattered. Some of them had gone to explore the trail, J. W. Black had taken a Pak-Jak and gone down to the mission, the others had been walking trying to reach one of the well-watered, palm-lined canyons we had seen from the air near the location of the mission.

According to the new and revised schedule we had been forced to adopt, we weren't going to have any more time to examine the country around the mission by helicopter. Emergency matters had necessitated my arrival at the ranch and the helicopter people had wired that Pete Rivas had to be in the Argentine within the next few days.

So Bob Boughton had to start rounding up the various people while the others started breaking camp.

It was quite a job.

Bob had to fly low over the trails until he would spot one of the men, then drop to a landing, pick the man up, bring him back to camp, then start off after another.

He came in with J. W. on one side of the helicopter and J. W.'s Pak-Jak strapped to the other side as balancing ballast. He found Ynes, David and Emery and gradually got the camp together. We left. The men were working like ants while we got in the helicopter and again started north to join Francisco and Pete, faced with the realization that there would be another inevitable delay while we were waiting for the pickups to catch up.

We made rendezvous with Pete and Francisco and then Bob and I took off to explore the country to the north and east, and particularly to see if we could get a close look at what Munoz had felt might well be the ruins of old buildings, including the ruin of one very large building.

It was interesting to note the precautions that were taken so that we could be located in case we had any trouble. Bob Boughton gave Pete and Francisco a series of bearings they could follow on the map in case we were not back by a certain time.

That trip that afternoon was one of the most interesting and eventful of all the trips I made on the entire expedition.

We flew high until we came to the place where Munoz had seen what he thought were buildings, and how Bob located the spot was a mystery to me.

This was a rugged, rough, scrambled terrain with ridges running in every conceivable direction. One section of the country, as far as I was concerned, looked just like any other section of the country. There was nothing I could see which could be used as a landmark, but Bob unerringly picked out the particular place we wanted and flew in low enough so that we could see unmistakably these were simply rocks which had been shaped by erosion so that the sides were straight up and down and the top of the largest rock had a certain dome-shaped appearance.

We hovered around and finally landed right on them.

I still can't understand the action of the erosion which had formed these rocks in this manner. Apparently there had been a stream which had followed a channel for many, many years and then for some reason had changed its channel and left some of the older channel high and dry. Then the more recent flow of water had cut across this old channel and carved the bedrock in perpendicular walls of perhaps some thirty feet in height.

Evidently there had been periods of storm when this stream ran with considerable force and carried a great volume of water.

I started exploring this watercourse and then came on something which was tremendously exciting: A place where the old channel of the stream had deposited some five or six feet of alluvial gravel on top of the old hardpan, then as the

Alluvial gravel deposited on top of bedrock, marking the old river channel. (After this gravel was deposited the river changed its course and cut down through the bedrock to a distance of some thirty feet. Since this country is rich in gold, the surface of the bedrock on this old channel probably holds quantities of placer gold.)

stream had changed its channel this hardpan had been cut down. The action must have gone on for thousands of years, because there were these perpendicular walls of hardpan some twenty or thirty feet in height and on top was the deposit of ancient alluvial gravel.

Since this "hardpan" was hard enough to furnish a bedrock for the old prehistoric stream and since this was a very rich gold-bearing country, it was certain that this old channel would have very considerable value. Perhaps fabulous value.

It was also apparent that with these perpendicular walls to be scaled and the alluvial gravel through which one must dig to come to the bedrock where the gold would be, the time element would not permit any exploration except with camera. I took some interesting pictures and subsequently when I showed those pictures to placer miners got quite a kick out of watching their tremendous excitement.

Apparently this is the type of discovery which a placer miner dreams about. Here was an old prehistoric channel with the bedrock exposed and sections of alluvial gravel lying on top of this bedrock which had been undisturbed for the thousands of years it had taken the new stream bed to cut down through the bedrock for a distance of some thirty feet.

This was, moreover, in a gold-bearing country of fabulous richness but the trouble had always been finding a place where bedrock was sufficiently shallow and level so that values could be recovered.

Juanito's story had been of finding a canyon in this country where the values were so fabulous that when he was still some forty feet above bedrock and had tunneled down below the surface to the depth of forty-two feet, he had simply by the use of bucket and windlass got more than a pound of gold within six weeks.

232

When one realizes that much of this time was consumed in digging through profitless overburden, in going some twelve miles for water and many more miles for provisions, that the pay dirt had to be hoisted out with a windlass from a forty foot shaft a bucket at a time and then put through a tedious dry-washing process, one can speculate that on the bedrock which Juanito estimated as being another forty to fifty feet deeper, the values would have been fabulous indeed.

However, we had very definitely promised that we would be back at the landing strip at El Marmol at a certain hour and we had no time to hunt for gold mines. We climbed back in the helicopter and Bob and I started for one other objective we had marked out — what seemed to be an interesting canyon with palm trees which Bob wanted to explore.

We were flying along over this country barely skimming the tops of the ridges and seeing things which it was impossible to detect from higher elevations — and there was plenty to be seen.

We came on a surprising waterfall and a huge water hole lined with grass in the midst of a barren canyon where there was not supposed to be any water. We couldn't resist putting the helicopter down briefly on this little oasis.

The water was slightly mineralized as it had a taste of baking soda but the pool was broad and deep and lined with a natural grass which quite evidently gave feed for wild game judging by the tracks and the trails leading to the water.

Here again we had no time for detailed exploration but had to content ourselves with a few hurried pictures and then start again for the landing strip at El Marmol.

Once more we came to a deep water hole in another canyon which looked so inviting we wanted to descend and

The last camp. Left to right: the author, Walter Moore, David Hurtado, J. W. Black and Pete Rivas. The helicopter is perched high on a granite rock.

explore but we had run out of time. We were then overdue at El Marmol and we realized the complications which could result if Munoz started a searching party and we should miss each other.

So we kept the helicopter in the air after hovering briefly over this new water hole, then went on to arrive at El Marmol just as the others were really beginning to worry about us.

Since Munoz was taking off for Tijuana and since night-flying over that country in a single-motored airplane is somewhat in the classification of playing Russian roulette, we knew that every additional minute we were taking in exploration was imposing great additional risk on Munoz — but I do wish we had had just an extra sixty minutes for exploration in that country.

However, we picked up Pete at the landing strip at El Marmol, Munoz took off into the late afternoon shadows for Tijuana and Pete, Bob and I went down the road to pick up the automobiles.

We found them at almost exactly the spot we had anticipated and made our last camp together.

Early the next morning Bob, Pete, Bob's wife, Jill, and I took off for the Hamilton Ranch, then for Ensenada, Tijuana, San Diego and home, a trip which was made without incident other than fighting a terrific head wind part of the time, turbulence part of the time and working under such a split-second schedule that we arrived at my ranch just about dark.

The next morning as Bob, Jill and Pete were taking off I suddenly realized that I had never fully ascertained what would have happened if we had had an engine failure over some of the rough country over which we had been flying.

I asked Bob about it and Bob said he could bring the helicopter down to a dead-stick landing without any trouble, although others had given me dire warnings of what would happen if the engine went dead.

So, deciding that I wanted to find out for myself exactly what would happen, I asked Bob to take me up some seven hundred feet over the ranch and shut off the engine.

We did this not only once but twice. I found out that, with this particular type of helicopter at least, it is just as easy to come down with a dead engine as it is with the engine running. At least I couldn't tell any difference.

So, our test completed, we again landed at the ranch. Bob, Jill and Pete got in the helicopter and for the last time we saw the whirlybird shoot straight up into the air, hover for an instant and then take off like a homing pigeon for the north.

11

How Deep the Canyons

I had expected that after a helicopter exploration of Baja California I would know all there was to know about it, I would have explored all the inaccessible canyons and would be satisfied.

I now realize that I have only scratched the surface.

I know that Baja California, at least the northern part of it, in place of being the barren, waterless desert it is supposed to be, is interspersed with numerous, palm-lined, well-watered canyons. I know that there are undiscovered water holes, that there are places where the possibility of making a rich gold strike is very great. I know that we have uncovered ruins which could well date back to the period when the Santa Ysabel Mission was supposed to have been constructed.

I know that two weeks by helicopter is utterly insufficient to explore the terrain satisfactorily and I know that as far as I am concerned Baja California is an even greater mystery than it ever was.

I have seen things no other writer has ever seen. I have

seen things perhaps no human being has ever seen within modern times. But I know that there is much more that I haven't seen and that under the blue, cloudless skies and the beating sunlight there are canyons where one could probably live in luxury if he had a weapon and ammunition, but where he would probably die of thirst if he tried to reach these canyons from any of the roads which have as yet been opened up.

In place of knowing Baja California intimately as I expected I would after this helicopter trip, I now realize that I hardly know it at all.

When we had first discovered the palm-lined canyons of La Asamblea and Sal Si Puede I had regarded them as a challenge. I wanted to get into them and explore. It was a conquer-Baja-California-or-bust sort of a feeling.

When we had finally managed to get into the canyons by Pak-Jak, there had been a lot of conversation about "conquering" the canyons.

We were brash and impudent and filled with a desire for adventure. The canyons had become an "objective" and we couldn't see anything except the canyons and "conquering the canyons."

Looking back on it now I realize that there is no such thing as "conquering" those canyons.

They were there long before we were born and they will be there long after we are dead. They remain silent, majestic, mysterious, flooded with sunlight, laced with streamers of gold ore, and deadly dangerous to the explorer who cannot keep up his lines of communication.

With a proper weapon and sufficient ammunition, with a relatively small amount of supplies, a resourceful man might well live in those canyons for a considerable period of time.

But he could never hope to get out alive once his line of communications had been severed.

As has been pointed out, establishing a line of communications in the first place is exceedingly difficult and maintaining it without the aid of equipment which is so expensive as to be out of all reason is a virtual impossibility.

Then a couple of nights after Bob, Jill and Pete had taken off in the helicopter, after some of my pictures had been developed, and "the gang" had gathered to look at colored photographs on the screen, I suddenly realized that while we hadn't "conquered" the canyons and could never expect to do so, the real advantage of the expedition had been something I had never thought about when I was concentrating on getting into these canyons and hovering over Baja California in a helicopter.

Over a period of many months while we had been planning how to get into the country, we had come to know each other better, to have the thrill of a friendship built on the cooperation necessary to achieve a group objective.

We had spent many nights around campfires. We had faced dangers together. We had planned and dreamed and had shared unusual experiences.

I had come to know Juanito with his unwavering loyalty to his ideals, his uncomplaining acceptance of conditions which would have driven most men to the depths of despondency. I had learned to appreciate Ynes, his keen eye, his indomitable energy, his remarkable outdoor ability.

And Francisco Munoz had turned out to be a companion, a pilot, and a friend. He had won such a place in my thoughts that as I look back on the trip I can realize many things I didn't understand at the time. Francisco knew that country and knew its dangers. He cheerfully handicapped his charter flying in order to be with us. During conditions of extreme turbulence he had worried about us even more than we had worried about ourselves.

And on that first trip when we had entered the canyons

when we knew that we were flirting with danger, when any unforeseen accident could have resulted in death, we could from time to time look up as we heard the drone of the engine on a plane, and there would be "Faithful Francisco" making a circle high overhead, studying the canyons and not returning to the course of his interrupted flight either north or south, as the case might have been, until he had satisfied himself we were all right.

Antero Diaz and his wife we had known before but while we were exploring the canyons we had come to know them much better. We had come to be virtually a part of the family, and Bahia de Los Angeles was no longer a place we visited as tourists. We had become a part of the community.

In short, my life had become much richer because of my association with these people.

The canyons lie there, bathed in sunlight during the daytime, silvered with moonlight at night. The various people who were actors in the drama of trying to explore these canyons go about their separate ways. At this writing Bob Boughton and Pete Rivas are in South America. Jill Boughton is working at her job in Palo Alto.

Murl Emery is back in the desert prospecting for a new mine, since his last mining deal blew up and "a million dollars went down the drain." (Everything had been there to make Emery a millionaire except that the material failed in one important test — a color test.)

But Emery is quite philosophical about it all. He didn't want money anyway, except that he *would* now like to buy a helicopter.

The Pak-Jak has attracted lots of attention. J. W. Black is working until late at night trying to keep up production. Lee Sine is in a spot where he has to think more of rationing deliveries than promoting sales.

Leo Roripaugh is running his ranch, coping with the

problems of a dry year. Dr. Westphal is once more deep in the problems of practicing medicine in a good-sized rural community — confinement cases, automobile accidents, emergency operations, an office overflowing with patients, night calls and all the rest of it.

My secretaries are running themselves ragged, filing mail, answering phones, transcribing records from my dictating machine.

But those long, mysterious, palm-lined canyons in Baja California have somehow intertwined our lives, strengthened our friendships and given us memories which have filled the storehouse of our thoughts with the treasures of life.

No matter how we may be separated in the future, those who were on the Baja California explorations forged bonds of friendships in the flickering light of the campfires, in the adventures and the dangers we shared.

Those canyons have enriched our lives. No one of us now thinks about "conquering" the canyons. They have introduced us to unforgettable experiences, have given us a new insight.

How deep are those canyons?

They are as deep as human experience, as human thought, as human companionship. They are as inscrutable as the desert itself, and as cruel. One mistake and a man could die in those canyons.

But they also have their benign side. They have exerted an influence on every one of us who looked on the waving palm fronds, heard the mysterious whisper of drifting sand on the wings of the night wind.

These are the things of which life is made: adventures, dangers, memories and friendships.

ERLE STANLEY GARDNER